MIGHTY HERCULES
The first four decades

MIGHTY HERCULES
The first four decades

Published by Royal Air Force
Benevolent Fund Enterprises,
Building 15, RAF Fairford,
Glos GL7 4DL, England
Publishing Director: Paul A. Bowen
Publishing Manager: Claire Lock

Written by: Lindsay Peacock
Managing Editor: Peter R. March
Contributing Authors: Julius Alexander, Sue Bushell, Joe Dabney and Tony Webb
Editorial Consultant: Bob Dutton
Photographs courtesy: Lockheed Aeronautical Systems Company
and as credited
Typeset & Design: Sue J. Bushell
Cover design: Graham Finch

ISBN 0 9516581 6 6

Typeset & Design: Sue J. Bushell
Cover design: Graham Finch

Paper courtesy: Interfor Limited
Printed in Hong Kong

CONTENTS

INTRODUCTION

On 23 August 1954, a new turboprop transport aircraft made its maiden flight at Burbank, California. In the 40 years since that auspicious occasion, the Lockheed C-130 has become a legend. The Hercules as it was soon to be named, presents no problems for anyone trying to sum up its achievements other than to run out of superlatives and space before running out of exploits to describe.

The Lockheed C-130, and its L-100 civil counterpart, has been almost everywhere from the Arctic to the Antarctic. It has landed on dirt strips . . . on snow and ice . . . on roads and even on an aircraft carrier. The Hercules has carried all sorts of cargo, from bombs and bullets in military conflicts around the world, to food and medicine on humanitarian relief operations. It has undertaken a greater variety of missions than almost any other type of aircraft, ranging from pure cargo-hauling through photo-mapping to in-flight refuelling and search-and-rescue. Perhaps most remarkable of all, the C-130 has been in continuous production at Marietta, Georgia for longer than any other type of aircraft in the western world.

That longevity provides testament to the `rightness' of the design in the first instance. Nevertheless, Lockheed has not been reluctant to incorporate changes at appropriate moments and this evolutionary process has undoubtedly helped to ensure a long production run. Today, the company and its Marietta work force stand on the brink of yet another change, but one that is spoken of as revolutionary, for the upcoming C-130J version is radically different from its predecessors and may fairly be called a Hercules for the next millennium.

In preparing this 40th anniversary tribute to the ubiquitous Lockheed C-130, the production team has not attempted to present a definitive history of the unique transport. Rather more, this is a celebration in words and pictures to provide a feel for what the Hercules is and what it does. It aims to give a flavour of its many achievements, by focusing on particular exploits and alluding briefly to others; and offers pointers to where the C-130 is heading, as it moves towards the 21st Century.

The editorial team – Lindsay Peacock, Sue Bushell and Peter R. March – is very grateful to Joseph E. Dabney, former Public Relations Co-ordinator of the Lockheed-Georgia Company, Wg Cdr Tony Webb AFC, RAF (Retd) and Julius Alexander, Communications Coordinator for Airlift, Lockheed Aeronautical Systems Company, Marietta for their significant contributions to this book. Their insight and input immeasurably improved the finished article, as did their permission to use first-hand accounts that initially appeared in other publications. Julius Alexander provided an invaluable liaison with the many people at LASC who checked through key parts of the text and the appendices. He also made available a large proportion of the uncredited photographs from the LASC files without which this volume would have been much the poorer.

Finally, the team would like to thank Bob Dutton, formerly with the Lockheed-Georgia Company and an enthusiastic friend of the RAF Benevolent Fund in his retirement. Bob has worked tirelessly over many months to assist the editorial team, first with the initial contacts and subsequently checking and advising on the final text. His enthusiasm has done much to keep the project on course to produce an appropriate tribute to the 'labours of Hercules' for its 40th birthday.

From Antarctica . . .

to the jungles of Vietnam . . .

and into the Gulf Desert . . .

. . . the Lockheed Hercules has been in its element.

BIRTH OF THE MIGHTY HERCULES

The first YC-130 to fly (53-3397) that was built at Burbank, California is seen here on its maiden flight on 23 August 1954.

The evolutionary process that culminated in the Lockheed C-130 had its origins in one war, although it was to be another war in the same part of the world that bore much of the responsibility for transforming the Hercules from being basically a transport aircraft into the flying equivalent of a 'jack of all trades'. If the C-130 can be said to have had its genesis in Korea, then Vietnam was surely at the root of its apotheosis.

That it was able to successfully meet the demands of so many differing tasks says much for the sound qualities inherent in the original design. There can be no doubt that whoever selected the name *Hercules* made a truly inspired choice. However, with all due respect to the hero of Greek mythology, there are some who would argue that the original Hercules had it easy, in as much as he was only called upon to perform 12 tasks, whereas the aircraft that now bears his name has undertaken many more labours over the course of a career which has spanned four decades and which shows no sign of ending.

The development of that aircraft effectively started within a few days of North Korea's June 1950 invasion of South Korea and had its origins in a Pentagon 'brain-storming' session tasked with preparing a package of ideas to make use of a $105 million supplement to the US Air Force's existing research and development budget. By all accounts, the personnel involved in that meeting ran out of ideas long before they ran out of money, at which point an unknown USAF Colonel – perhaps exasperated at having to work over the weekend – uttered a mild expletive and followed up with a remark to the effect that what the Air Force really needed was a rugged medium transport capable of carrying a 30,000lb payload of freight or troops over a distance of about 1,500 miles and with the ability to operate safely from unimproved surfaces.

It was a tall order, but debate on this interesting idea seems to have been less concerned with technical merits than financial ones, apparently focusing more on the question of just how much money should be allocated. In the event, a figure was agreed and an unspecified sum of money in the low millions of dollars was set aside for study of a 'medium tactical transport'. Shortly afterwards, the budget request was sent on its way through the appropriations treadmill, where it survived and prospered to provide the impetus that ultimately led to the YC-130.

Events were placed on a more official footing at the beginning of 1951 when Tactical Air Command (TAC) undertook a number of studies which examined the airlift mission in considerably more exhaustive detail. Within a few weeks, the rather nebulous idea advocated by an unknown colonel had evolved into a much firmer concept that allowed USAF Headquarters to issue a formal General Operational Requirement (GOR) on 2 February 1951, simultaneously inviting key aerospace manufacturing companies such as Boeing, Douglas, Fairchild and Lockheed to respond to the Request for Proposals (RFP).

In the previous few months, aware of developments in the Pentagon, Lockheed had attempted to steal a march on its competitors and had been giving serious thought to developing a new transport aircraft for military use. To that end, company engineering and sales personnel had embarked on a round of visits to senior personnel in USAF Headquarters at the Pentagon. In addition, they went to the Fort Bragg/Pope AFB complex in North Carolina to learn something about the needs of individuals at the 'sharp end' of the tactical airlift mission, as well as to observe airdrop operations at first hand.

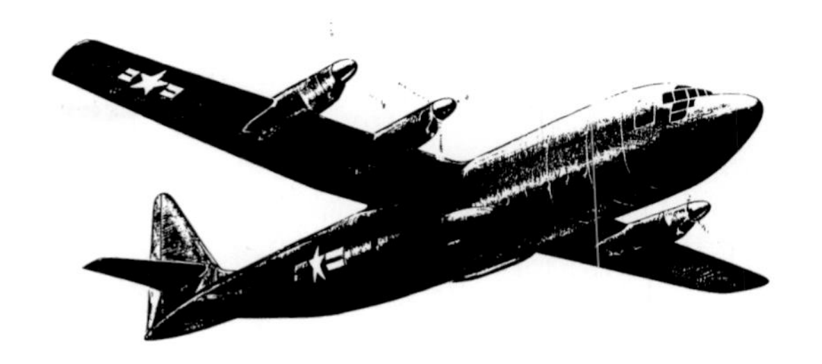

An artists' impression of the preliminary L-206 design of 1951.

So, in February 1951, when the RFP was issued, Lockheed was reasonably well prepared to respond to what was a pretty tough requirement. Broadly speaking, it invited design submissions for a medium transport capable of undertaking tactical and logistical airlift duties. In those terms, it sounds fairly straightforward, but the requirement stipulated that the new aircraft must also possess strategic applications and these did not always sit comfortably with the tactical mission.

Essentially, it was to be able to airlift up to 90 troops over 2,000-mile stage lengths, but still retain the potential to operate almost independently from rough and ready landing fields close to the front line. It should be relatively speedy, in order to minimise transit time on long over-water flights, such as between the USA and Europe or the Far East. It should also be capable of controlled flight at slow speeds, so as to safely perform the airdropping of troops and supplies by parachute. It should be able to accommodate all sorts of items of equipment, ranging from packages of medical supplies right up to some of the larger Army artillery pieces. In short, it should be flexible and sophisticated, but simple and robust enough to be equally at home on well appointed air bases and unpaved dirt strips. It was, in anybody's book, a tall order to fulfil.

With the new transport having moved a stage closer to becoming reality, Lockheed's Burbank-based Advanced Design Department, headed by Willis Hawkins, got down to some serious work on preparing its submission, which was given the temporary designation L-206. Responsibility for leading the preliminary design team was entrusted to Art Flock, who subsequently moved across country to head the engineering effort at Marietta. He eventually rose to the position of Vice-President of the Lockheed-Georgia Division.

Other individuals associated with the project included Al Lechner, who looked after matters relating to the general configuration; Jack Lebold, who concerned himself with the undercarriage; and Willard Tjossen and Merrill Kelly, who were involved with engine selection and installation. For once, the formidable and forthright Kelly Johnson was not directly involved, although that did not prevent him from voicing his opinions at a 1952 unveiling of a model of the proposed transport. This, however, proved to be one of the rare occasions when he seems to have got it wrong.

Further consultations with TAC and the US Army as well as the Military Air Transport Service (MATS) were a necessary part of the design process, since there was little point in venturing to the drawing board without a clear and concise understanding of exactly what the customer wanted. Various avenues were explored and rejected before the design was firmed up and submitted to the Air Force in April 1951.

The Model L-206 was nothing, if not radical, forsaking tried and generally trusted piston propulsion for the still relatively unproven but potentially much more reliable turboprop. And four of them at that, Lockheed having agonized long and hard over the powerplant installation before electing to go for four engines in order to satisfy stringent engine-out criteria. Nor was it at all elegant, its workmanlike lines centering around a low-slung, fuselage with a sharply upswept aft section capped by a huge fin; bulbous undercarriage fairings and a plank-like wing structure. As for the cockpit, this had a horticultural appearance, for its 23 windows made it resemble a greenhouse where one might reasonably expect to grow tomatoes.

Even though it may have lacked the graceful lines of other Lockheed products, those who were responsible for evaluating the four contenders evidently recognised the Model L-206's inherent potential and it was duly adjudged as the winner. Official acknowledgement of that fact came on 2 July 1951, little more than a year from the start of the hostilities in Korea and just five months after the RFP was released to industry. Things clearly moved fast in those days.

For Lockheed, winning the contest and securing a contract for two YC-130 prototypes was merely the end of the beginning. Many more obstacles had to be overcome before the Hercules took its place on the flight-lines at the air bases that were home to TAC's Troop Carrier Wings.

The first steps along that path were taken within a few weeks of the US Air Force go-ahead, when work began on manufacture of the two prototypes in hangar C-1 at Burbank in August 1951. As it turned out, these were destined to be the only examples of the Hercules to be produced in California, for the decision was soon taken to locate any full-scale production that might ensue at Marietta, Georgia, using the facilities of Air Force Plant Six.

The first YC-130 getting airborne at Burbank on 23 August 1954 with Stan Beltz and Roy Wimmer at the controls.

One of the photographs taken of the YC-130 as it neared Edwards AFB on its first flight.

This aircraft plant was established in World War 2 specifically to build the B-29, with almost 700 examples being completed before the end of hostilities resulted in closure of the line. The factory buildings were then used for storage for a number of years, until Lockheed arrived during January 1951, initially to refurbish 120 B-29s for service with the Air Force and eventually as one of three production centres for the Boeing B-47. Just under 400 Stratojets were completed by Lockheed during the period 1953-57, but that effort pales into insignificance when compared with the amount of energy that has been expended on the Hercules programme though 40 continuous (and continuing) years of production.

Little more than a year after the decision to proceed to the prototype stage, the USAF gave the company and project a tremendous boost when, on 19 September 1952, it issued a letter contract calling for an initial production batch of seven aircraft. Three days later, with the entire programme on a much more secure footing, Lockheed-Georgia personnel, headed by Al Brown, began arriving in California in order to smooth the transfer of design and engineering responsibility across to Marietta, Georgia

For the moment, though, events in California took priority, with manufacture and assembly of the two prototypes forging ahead steadily throughout 1953 and on into 1954. The latter year was significant in a number of ways, not least of which were contracts for follow-on production batches. The first of these came in April, when the Air Force 'upped the ante' yet again with an order for 20 more aircraft. That figure was eclipsed in September by the purchase of 48 more, raising planned procurement of the initial C-130A model to 75.

An equally significant event in 1954 was of course the maiden flight. In fact, this actually preceded placing of the second order and took place on 23 August, with company test pilots Stan Beltz and Roy Wimmer at the controls and flight engineers Jack Real and Dick Stanton also present in the cockpit. Morning smog in the vicinity of the Burbank plant prevented the planned take-off time of 0900 hr. The delay lasted until well into the afternoon. Eventually, the sun managed to penetrate the gloom and conditions quickly improved thereafter, to the point where it was decided to go ahead. Beltz and his three colleagues were soon on board the second YC-130 (53-3397) and busy with final preparations.

Before long, there came the now familiar sound of Allison T56 turboprop engines starting up and after a few final checks that all was well, Beltz released the brakes and carefully guided the YC-130 towards the runway. Lining up, he advanced the throttles and the aircraft began moving, picking up speed quickly as it accelerated down the runway. Beltz eased back on the control column and raised the nose momentarily before allowing it to settle back down again as he called for reverse thrust. Rolling out to the far end of the runway, Beltz turned the YC-130 and repeated the manoeuvre in the opposite direction, before waiting a few moments while a couple of chase aircraft got airborne.

Once they were safely out of the way, the YC-130 again took the active runway, the whine of its engines increasing in intensity as full power was applied. For a few seconds it remained almost motionless as Beltz held it on the brakes, prompting some ground observers to speak of it 'dancing a jig', as if it was impatient with all the waiting around and eager to be airborne. Then, at precisely 1445hr, Beltz freed it from its restraint and gave the machine its head. Eight seconds later, he smoothly pulled the control column back and YC-130 53-3397 left the ground for the first time, after a take-off roll using just 855ft of tarmac.

Continuing with the climb to an altitude of about 10,000ft, the flight crew then set about completing the few test objectives that had been scheduled for the sortie. These included a preliminary control and handling assessment, some stall checks, and cycling of the undercarriage and flap assemblies. Everything worked almost exactly as advertised. The opportunity was then taken to rendezvous with a camera ship for some air-to-air photography, before steering a course that would take the YC-130 over the Sierra Nevada mountain range to a landing at Edwards AFB, California after 61 minutes in the air.

There, amidst the euphoria that invariably surrounds the completion of a maiden flight, those most intimately associated with the programme probably enjoyed a brief respite from the pressure. Tomorrow and succeeding days might well bring trials and tribulations, but today was a time for celebration and congratulation at successfully negotiating the first of many important milestones.

Meanwhile, work carried on remorselessly at Marietta, where the first few production examples were beginning to take shape and where General Manager Dan Haughton kept everyone associated with the Hercules project very much on their toes. A dynamic and hugely popular leader, Haughton chose not to isolate himself in his office. He opted instead for a 'hands-on' style of management, finding time to make daily visits to the production floor, engineering facilities and flight line. While his brisk approach may occasionally have resulted in ruffled feathers amongst his colleagues, those same colleagues recognised his intense desire to make the Georgia operation a permanent star in the Lockheed firmament. That desire rubbed off on almost everyone he came into contact with, paying handsome dividends in terms of loyalty and determination to succeed.

It all started to come together in 1955, a year which was rather a roller-coaster ride for the Marietta team. As the year opened the pair of YC-130 prototypes were still at Edwards AFB, California, but the development effort took a big stride forward on 12 January when the second Marietta-built aircraft (53-3130) was assigned to static test duties. A key aspect of this involved verifying that the structure was up to the job being asked of it. This required the company to demonstrate that the cabin was able to cope with pressures of up to 15lb per sq in – or twice the normal operating limit.

Initially, this involved a certain amount of hazard, for pressurisation trials were undertaken in one of the Marietta hangars and failure could have been quite literally an explosive situation. Later, making use of British experience and expertise in fatigue and pressure testing arising from the Comet airliner disasters, Lockheed became the first US company to utilise the much safer hydrostatic method. It invested in a pair of water tanks, one to be used for small assemblies – the other a much more ambitious rig in which the entire fuselage of 53-3130 was immersed and eventually tested to destruction after completing the equivalent of four full life-cycles.

While the static test effort was vital, it was conducted well away from the public gaze, but activities at Marietta received a welcome shot of publicity on 10 March 1955 when the first production machine (53-3129) was rolled out amidst a certain amount of pomp and ceremony. Senior company officials, US Air Force officers and local dignitaries such as the Georgia state Governor Marvin Griffin, were in attendance. In fact, it was the latter individual who was invited to christen the aircraft with a bottle of water drawn

The two prototype YC-130s remained test flying at Edwards AFB through 1955.

from the nearby Chattahoochee River. Four determined attempts were needed before Griffin managed to smash the bottle, prompting the inevitable remark, 'You also build tough airplanes'. Just how tough soon became apparent.

Four weeks after the roll-out, a much more significant event took place, with the maiden flight of C-130A 53-3129 on 7 April. On this occasion, company pilots Bud Martin and Leo Sullivan were at the controls when the aircraft broke ground in the late morning, after an even shorter take-off roll than that used by the YC-130 less than eight months earlier. Systems checks kept them fairly busy during the sortie, but they found time to perform a couple of fly-bys for the benefit of ground observers before landing.

Confidence was high in the aftermath of the successful first flight, but was to take a severe jolt on the aircraft's third sortie one week later. This 131-minute trip was, in fact, the first data-gathering mission. Everything had gone almost flawlessly throughout, with the various objectives including propeller feathering, air-starting all four engines and a short air-to-air photography session, before ending with a number of calibration runs at speeds ranging from 95 to 150kt.

Leo Sullivan was in command on this occasion, with Art Hansen occupying the co-pilot seat and Bob Brennan acting as the flight engineer. Also on board to monitor the aircraft's performance were engineers Lloyd Frisbee, Ed Shockley and Carroll Fruth. The latter was feeling decidedly unwell as the C-130A bounced about in unstable air while making a succession of low passes over the Marietta airfield. After enduring almost 30 minutes of this torture, Fruth wanted nothing more than to get back to terra firma and the prospect of relief must have been very sweet as Sullivan configured the aircraft for landing.

Above: The Governor of Georgia, Marvin Griffin, manages at the fourth attempt to 'christen' the first production C-130A (53-3129) on 10 March 1955. Below: Governor Griffin (right) was joined by Don Haughton and Col Edward J. McRay Jnr for the naming ceremony.

It was as the C-130A turned on to a short final approach leg that Ed Shockley's attention was drawn to the overhead panel where he noticed the number two engine fuel tank boost pump indicator flicker. This was the first intimation of a problem, but the signal was indistinct and Shockley chose to remain silent during the critical moments leading up to touch-down. The ensuing landing was accomplished normally and reverse thrust was selected almost immediately to slow the aircraft to taxiing speed.

At that moment, Carroll Fruth – who was occupying the airborne observer's station in the hold – observed the number two engine tachometer go haywire and begin to

The first production C-130A made its maiden flight on 7 April 1955 at Marietta.

unwind rapidly, whereupon he rose from his seat to peer out through one of the fuselage windows. A tongue of flame was immediately apparent at the rear of the inner nacelle, but even as he watched, the entire engine was engulfed by fire.

In the cockpit, alerted by Fruth's shout of alarm, Sullivan and the flight deck crew were shutting down the port engines and activating the fire extinguisher system, while struggling to bring the still-moving aircraft to a halt. As far as the fire was concerned, their efforts failed to achieve the desired effect. Indeed, it took even firmer hold and within a few moments more was raging well out of control. Shutting down the two starboard engines and cutting off remaining electrical power, Sullivan eventually had no option but to give the order to abandon the aircraft, which everyone managed to do safely, even though the crew exit was adjacent to the blazing engine.

Smart work by the Dobbins Air Force Base fire service, which was quickly on the scene, brought the fire under control within 10 minutes. Indeed, their work was instrumental in saving the aircraft, not only to fly again, but also to assist the ensuing investigation which quickly pinpointed the cause of the fire. Smothered in foam and with the port wing having melted and broken away inboard of the inner engine, the once pristine C-130 was now a very sorry sight indeed and an atmosphere of gloom soon pervaded the Georgia division as news of the catastrophe spread through the work force. About the only note of optimism concerned the fact that the accident had not claimed any lives, all of those most intimately associated with the Hercules acknowledging that Lockheed had been very fortunate.

Within hours, study of the accident isolated the probable culprit and it did not take too much more time to determine the precise cause and effect a permanent cure. The problem had stemmed from the failure to correctly secure a quick disconnect fitting on a fuel line. From that point on, it was fundamentally an 'accident waiting to happen'. A combination of turbulence and vibration experienced in flight eventually resulted in the coupling working loose and separating. This in turn led to a serious leak of fuel, which ignited soon after touch-down and very nearly caused the total loss of the aircraft.

As for 53-3129, following diagnosis of the cause of the fire, it was returned to the factory for work that included fitting a replacement wing. Following repair, it made its second 'maiden flight' on 6 February 1956 and eventually went on to enjoy a particularly illustrious career, spending time with the Eastern Test Range on missile tracking tasks and later seeing combat in South-East Asia after being modified to AC-130A gunship configuration.

If the accident involving the first Georgia-built aircraft was the nadir of 1955, then a compensatory high point undoubtedly came on 10 August, when the USAF clearly demonstrated its continuing faith in the Lockheed machine by placing its fourth contract for the production article. The latest buy was also destined to be one of the largest single purchases, for it covered a total of 84 aircraft, which more than doubled the number on order to 159.

Despite that welcome development, 1955 brought other problems and none appeared more intractable than the mismatch between engine and propeller. This, in fact, was not strictly a problem that came within Lockheed's domain and should really have been left to the Air Force and Curtiss-Wright to resolve. However, it certainly affected Lockheed and for a time seemed sufficiently serious in nature to threaten cancellation. Consequently, Lockheed expended a considerable amount of energy in trying to make the pairing work.

Basically, it stemmed from poor performance of the Curtiss-Wright turbo-electric propeller. It frequently over-compensated on the pitch setting in response to electrical signals, which resulted in the propeller 'snatching' and the engine surging. This resulted in what can best be described as a bumpy ride. Determined efforts to overcome the problem failed to achieve the desired results and eventually

Just after the aircraft (53-3129) touched down at Dobbins AFB on its third flight a major fire at the back of No. 2 engine caused substantial damage to its port wing.

After its repair the aircraft (53-3129) made its second maiden flight on 6 February 1956.

The first production C-130A went on to be used as a JC-130A (above) at the Eastern Test Range and was subsequently converted to an AC-130A gunship (below).

prompted the Air Force to direct a change to hydraulically-actuated propellers manufactured by Aeroproducts.

Testing of this component on the Hercules began with the sixth aircraft in late November 1955. The revised engine and propeller combination demonstrated superior reliability characteristics during the course of a trials project that lasted until early in July 1956. In the meantime, production of the Hercules had continued – to the point where Lockheed had close to 50 aircraft lying around immobile as they waited for the Air Force to make up its mind on the propeller question. Once it did, these machines were quickly retrofitted with Aeroproducts units.

With more aircraft available during late 1955 and throughout 1956, the pace of testing accelerated as Lockheed

Line-up of early C-130As on the south (Naval Air Station) side of the Lockheed/Dobbins/Atlanta NAS facility. Note the old style nose-wheel doors and in the background a Lockheed-built B-47 Stratojet.

and Air Force personnel sought to establish just what the C-130 could and could not do. This naturally involved several different stages, some of which were concerned with 'extending the envelope' in terms of performance, while others examined operational suitability in a variety of environments.

The first two stages were accomplished with the YC-130 prototypes and were fairly brief efforts in which the aircraft were operated to about 80% of design limits. Phase I was accomplished by company test pilots, while Phase II was essentially a verification exercise using Air Force personnel. The focus of the test work then shifted to contractor development (Phase III) which was intended to identify and then eliminate any 'glitches', as a precursor to Phase IV performance and stability trials in which the entire performance range was explored.

At this stage several aircraft were busy with the remaining development objectives. These comprised all-weather testing (Phase V); functional development using a number of production airframes (Phase VI); operational suitability with pilots from the designated user command, in this case TAC (Phase VII) and, finally, unit operational employment under the supervision of the Air Proving Ground Command (Phase VIII).

As development progressed, so did the number of locations supporting the test effort also rise, to a point where several different establishments were involved. Lockheed's production centre at Marietta was one, but the Air Force contribution was accomplished on a much broader basis. The Air Force Flight Test Center at Edwards AFB, California naturally played a leading role, particularly with regard to exploring performance.

All-weather trials were a prime responsibility of personnel of the Air Proving Ground Command at Eglin AFB, Florida. Some of this work involved using laboratory facilities, but test-dedicated aircraft were also despatched to other

Remaining in service for over 30 years, C-130As were modified with four-blade propellers and some had the 'Pinocchio' nose of later models. This had not been given to the 27th production aircraft when it visited RAF Greenham Common in 1979.
PHOTO: PETER R MARCH

locations for practical assessment of operating from high altitude airports in high temperature conditions ('hot-and-high') and cold weather trials. Eglin also had a key role to play in exploring rough-field capabilities as the Hercules was thoroughly evaluated on unprepared strips situated in the huge expanse of real estate that comprised the Florida test base. These quickly verified that the Lockheed machine was indeed almost a 'go-anywhere' aircraft.

On the other side of the country, the National Parachute Test Range facility at El Centro was the principal location for the first air drop experiments. These proved that the C-130 was able to perform aerial resupply tasking. A more prolonged series of paradrops and assault landings was later undertaken at Pope AFB, North Carolina, using equipment and troops from the 82nd Airborne Division which occupied the adjacent Army encampment at Fort Bragg.

For the most part, these trials revealed few difficulties. One that took time to resolve related to the undercarriage, which proved reluctant to operate on a number of occasions. A 'fix' was eventually worked out, but the stubborn defect necessitated at least one 'wheels-up' landing being made during the course of 1956. Embarrassingly for Lockheed and the Air Force, this incident occurred during an air drop at Fort Bragg which was subject to on-board observation by a team of Army colonels whose job it was to report on air drop systems.

Having safely deposited paratroops, Major Russ Dobyns, the pilot in command, headed back to Pope, only to find that the undercarriage refused to lower, even using manual methods. Efforts to fix the problem continued while the aircraft orbited to consume fuel but these proved unsuccessful and eventually there was no option but to perform a wheels-up landing on a foam-covered runway. As if that was not bad enough, a sudden wind-shift forced a last-minute change in landing direction and for a few moments Dobyns was uncertain as to whether enough fuel remained. Happily, it did, and the ensuing landing was safely accomplished, with the Army colonels evidently commenting later that they noticed little or no difference from a normal landing. That may well have been a deliberate understatement, for the touch-down was probably somewhat noisier than usual, since the aircraft skidded on its belly for more than 1,000ft before coming to a halt.

Thankfully, no fire resulted and the extent of the damage was minimal. Application of a temporary sheet metal patch over the damaged area allowed the C-130 to be flown to Marietta the next day for repairs. Within about 10 days, a new skin had been applied and the aircraft was back in action, apparently none the worse for its adventures.

Mishaps of that kind were, however, few and far between and the development phase was completed with the minimum of fuss. Some re-engineering was necessary, particularly with regard to the horizontal tail surfaces, where predicted load distribution was at variance with reality, resulting in buckling of the leading edge in certain flight regimes. On the C-130A, this was overcome by enforcing a maximum speed limit, but with effect from the C-130B an engineering change resulted in increased stiffness being built in to eliminate any possibility of a recurrence.

Data gained during flight testing revealed that Lockheed had handsomely exceeded performance goals as stipulated by the original US Air Force requirement. Indeed, the figures were remarkable, for the C-130 cruised 20% faster; had a ceiling and rate of climb that were 35% better; and cut take-off and landing distances by 25% and 40% respectively.

Just as welcome for the crews who would soon introduce it to operational service with Tactical Air Command was the fact that it was fun to fly, with plenty of power in reserve and admirable controllability, unlike the lumbering Fairchild C-119s that they were used to. Not surprisingly, they looked forward to getting their hands on Lockheed's latest product with a great deal of eagerness – and the entire programme took a huge step forward on 9 December 1956 when the first examples to be assigned to an operational unit were formally delivered to TAC's 463rd Troop Carrier Wing at Ardmore AFB, Oklahoma.

The ninth production C-130A (54-1622) visiting Ardmore AFB, Oklahoma in 1956.

WORK-HORSE

A Tactical Air Command Hercules (322nd Air Division) in its original red and silver paint scheme.

The first example of the Hercules to be delivered to a Tactical Air Command (TAC) unit was the 50th aircraft to be built at Marietta, with C-130A 55-0023 leaving its birthplace and heading north-west to its new home at Ardmore AFB, Oklahoma on 9 December 1956. Waiting to greet it and four other aircraft that were flown in that day was a crowd of around 5,000 people, headed by TAC's commanding officer, General O. P. Weyland, who officially accepted the *City of Ardmore* (as it had been named for the occasion) from the then chairman of Lockheed, Robert E. Gross.

Once the fanfare of publicity died down, the 463rd Troop Carrier Wing (TCW) got down to the serious business of completing the re-equipment process and becoming intimately acquainted with its new mount. Aircraft came in thick and fast. The propeller problems alluded to in the previous chapter had resulted in a log-jam at Marietta while Lockheed and the Air Force sought a solution. Now, with the Aeroproducts unit having been selected to replace the troublesome Curtiss Turbo-Electric units, Lockheed was quick to retrofit the new propellers and deliver the finished aircraft.

A second unit also took delivery of its first C-130A before the end of 1956. This was the 314th TCW at Sewart AFB, Tennessee and, like the 463rd, conversion to the Hercules was accompanied by the loss of one squadron. Henceforth, both outfits were three-squadron organisations, with each possessing about 50 examples of the Hercules.

While the number of aircraft on hand was reduced, productivity certainly did not suffer as a consequence, for the Allison turboprop powerplants of the C-130A meant that it could zip along at a considerably greater speed than the lumbering piston-powered C-119 Flying Boxcars it replaced. In addition, it could also accommodate a significantly increased payload, whether it be of men or material. Small wonder that both units formed an integral part of TAC's Composite Air Strike Force (CASF), nor did they have to wait too long before the call to action came.

Having completed equipping its planned force of six US-based squadrons, attention then shifted to overseas-based commands in the European and Pacific theatres. Each of these was also destined to acquire the Hercules as a replacement for the C-119. The process started with the United States Air Forces in Europe (USAFE). The first C-130A to be deployed in Europe was delivered to the 317th TCW at Evreux-Fauville, France in early September 1957. Sufficient examples were eventually received to equip three squadrons. From the very start the Hercules made its presence felt, bringing a new dimension to routine and not-so-routine airlift duties in support of operations over an area extending from the Persian Gulf in the east to the United Kingdom in the west.

On the other side of the world, in Japan, the first sighting of the new tactical transport occurred in December 1957, when a single TAC machine was despatched to the region for the dual purposes of surveying routes and assessing infrastructure at the bases from which it was destined to operate. As with USAFE, the Pacific Air Forces (PacAF) command was to possess a single C-130A wing (the 483rd TCW at Ashiya AB, Japan) with which to satisfy in-theatre airlift requirements.

Re-equipment began in earnest in early 1958, affecting two squadrons that operated from Ashiya itself as well as a third that was stationed at Tachikawa, on the outskirts of Tokyo. The latter moved to Naha, Okinawa during November 1958. Subsequently, in June 1960, the closure of Ashiya and concurrent inactivation of the 483rd TCW led to adoption of a scheme whereby operational control of the three squadrons was assigned to the 315th Air Division, which was responsible for overseeing all theatre airlift from its headquarters at Tachikawa. Henceforth, one squadron resided at Tachikawa, with the other two situated at Naha, where they were particularly conveniently placed to furnish airlift support throughout PacAF's huge area of responsibility.

By a stroke of good fortune, the first 18 months or so of operational service coincided with a rare period of stability in global affairs, affording the USAF a welcome calm in which to deploy its new tactical airlifter at home and abroad. In the spring of 1958, however, storm clouds were beginning to gather at a number of potential flash-points on opposite sides of the world. For the Hercules and its crews, these would soon present the chance to demonstrate their mettle.

The first such opportunity came in May 1958 when the safety of Vice-President Richard Nixon appeared to be threatened by the presence of unruly mobs during a visit to Caracas, Venezuela. With the benefit of hindsight, there are some who might argue that subsequent US history would have been better served if Nixon had been left to fend for himself, but President Dwight D. Eisenhower wasted little time in ordering almost 600 paratroops of the 101st Airborne Division at Fort Campbell, Kentucky to be flown to Puerto Rico and stand ready to intervene should a rescue attempt be deemed necessary.

Sewart's 314th TCW drew the 'short straw' on this occasion, with most of its fleet of aircraft taking part in the airlift operation. In addition to troops, a considerable amount of equipment was also ferried to Puerto Rico. Jeeps, trucks, ambulances, artillery pieces, ammunition, fuel and even a helicopter were among the loads flown 1,600 miles to the Caribbean island. Once the crisis had blown over, Nixon had departed and stability had been restored, they were then flown 1,600 miles back again.

Two months later a much more serious situation arose in the Middle East. This was the Lebanon crisis of July 1958,

The 463rd Troop Carrier Wing from Ardmore AFB operated from Ashiya AB, Japan during the Taiwan Straits crisis.

when the revolution in Iraq prompted President Chamoun to call upon the USA for assistance in forestalling the risk of a similar event in his small state. By coincidence TAC forces were engaged in *Trade Wind*, a CASF quick-reaction exercise, when the crisis broke in mid-July. The command was thus able to mobilise resources for Task Force 'Bravo' more or less immediately. Within 24 hours, the first Super Sabres had arrived in Turkey, vanguard of a force that eventually grew to number around 100 tactical fighter and bomber aircraft.

At the same time, Marine ground forces were wading ashore at Beirut and a near-armada of C-130As was heading towards the Middle East from bases in Europe and the USA. On board were 24th Infantry Division troops to bolster the garrison in Lebanon, technicians and engineers to service TAC fighter and bomber assets at the deployment bases in Turkey and all sorts of other equipment necessary to support forces in the field. It was easily the most significant test of the C-130's capability to date and the Hercules performed sterling work in carrying the majority of the eight million pounds of equipment moved during the 11-day airlift.

Even as the situation in the Lebanon cooled off, TAC and the Hercules wings faced a fresh challenge in a very different part of the world. In the Far East, the People's Republic of China (PRC) had long made use of loudspeakers to harangue the Nationalist Chinese on the islands of Quemoy and Matsu. Now, no longer content with aiming a verbal barrage across the narrow waters of the Formosa Straits, PRC forces switched to heavy artillery and began lobbing shells instead, possibly as a preliminary to assault landings and full-blown warfare.

Bombardment began with a particularly intense barrage on 23 August and continued thereafter at a diminished rate. The aggressive action very quickly extended to the use of air power, with MiG-17s undertaking strafing missions against the outlying islands on the 24th. Eventually, facing an ever-worsening crisis, President Eisenhower acted. Again, US naval reinforcements were hastening to the region and a TAC Composite Air Strike Force was in the forefront, with fighter and attack aircraft moving swiftly across the Pacific to bases on Taiwan, Okinawa, Japan and the Philippines. As would be increasingly the case in months and years to come, the Hercules did not lag far behind.

When the Taiwan crisis erupted, the Ashiya-based 483rd TCW still had quite a long way to go to complete the task of transition from the C-119 to the C-130 and was far from combat-ready. Nevertheless, it was able to make a notable contribution to the airlift of personnel and equipment to Taiwan in the initial stages of the crisis. So, not surprisingly, did elements of both US-based Troop Carrier Wings.

In fact, the 463rd TCW already had eight aircraft and about 140 personnel in place at Ashiya, on what had started out as the first temporary duty (TDY) period at an overseas base by a C-130 unit. Those resources comprised a detachment from the 772nd Troop Carrier Squadron, which had deployed from Ardmore at the beginning of March for the express purpose of aiding in the 483rd's conversion. They were soon put to good use assisting with the transfer of men

Paratroopers jump from the ramp of a C-130A using a static line.

RC-130A 57-0524 became part of the Air Force Communications Service fleet. PHOTO: LINDSAY PEACOCK

line radar sites. Located in the Arctic, these were fundamentally the first line of defence against surprise attack by Soviet bomber forces and it was therefore vital to maintain good supply links if they were to remain fully operational at all times.

Not surprisingly, a series of tests was undertaken before the USAF decided to proceed with procurement of the 'Ski-bird'. These were accomplished with the 48th production C-130A (55-0021) in 1957 and included operations from a landing site at Bemidji, Minnesota which confirmed that the ski-equipped Hercules could be successfully adapted for use in such a hostile environment.

Subsequently, it was decided to complete a dozen aircraft in the definitive 'Ski-bird' configuration from an existing C-130A contract. These were handed over to the 314th TCW's 61st Troop Carrier Squadron at Sewart in the latter half of 1958. Transfer to a new squadron (the 17th TCS) at Dyess AFB, Texas came in early 1961, but these distinctive machines were eventually based at Elmendorf AFB, Alaska with effect from June 1964, remaining there until 1975 when they were reassigned to the New York Air National Guard unit at Schenectady.

The second new-build derivative that was based on the original 'A' model was a version optimised for photo-mapping duties with the Military Air Transport Service (MATS). In fact, the RC-130A (as it was designated) marked the end of manufacture of the basic C-130A family in 1959, but by then at least two other variations had appeared as a result of post-production modification projects.

Foremost amongst these was the C-130A-II which was soon deployed to Frankfurt, from where it gathered electronic intelligence relating to the nearby Warsaw Pact nations of Eastern Europe. This was a mission that was not without hazard, as the shooting down of one aircraft with the loss of 17 crew by Soviet fighters on 2 September 1958 confirms. Although this machine was apparently flying on the Turkish side of the border, it may have unwittingly strayed into the Soviet Union. Either way, the wreckage ended up near Sasunashen, Armenia.

Another early modification effort resulted in the appearance of the DC-130A drone launch and control platform and a number of early production aircraft were used to track missiles as JC-130As. Such modification efforts clearly confirmed that the Hercules was capable of performing missions that were far removed from conventional airlift. While that may have been encouraging news for Lockheed, there can be little doubt that the manufacturer was obviously far more interested in ensuring a long production run and securing a stable financial future for itself.

Improvements were made to the C-130A in the late 1950s including re-engining with more powerful Allison T-56-A-7 turboprop engines and four-bladed propellers. Internal fuel capacity was also increased.. PHOTO: PETER R. MARCH

Most of the 156 C-130B production aircraft went to Tactical Air Command.

The appearance of the next major model shortly before the end of 1958 was to be a major step in the right direction. In general appearance it did not look so very different from the C-130A, but it was markedly superior in several ways, not least of which was the adoption of more powerful Allison T56-A-7 turboprop engines. Rated at 4,050-eshp, these were married to four-bladed Hamilton Standard propellers, which were installed on all subsequent versions and later retrofitted to many C-130As. Other improvements included extra internal fuel capacity and a more robust undercarriage. The net result of these alterations was an increase of slightly over 10,000lb in gross operating weight, which rose to 135,000lb. This did not actually translate into increased payload capacity, but benefits were gained with regard to field performance and range.

The C-130B may fairly be said to have paved the way for the massive orders secured by later versions. If derivatives are taken into account the total production run was remarkably similar to the 'A' model, with some 230 examples of the C-130B family being completed by Lockheed between 1958 and 1963, as compared with 231 C-130As. Not surprisingly, the bulk of production was of the airlift-dedicated C-130B. A total of 156 examples was completed to this standard. Most went to TAC, but it also found acceptance internationally, with five overseas air arms accounting for about 30 aircraft between them. That may sound pretty insignificant against the 450-plus foreign sales achieved by the C-130H family to the present date, but it was a start – and word soon began to spread to other potential military customers that the Hercules was a rather useful piece of equipment to have in the inventory.

The KC-130F in-flight refuelling tanker for the US Marine Corps was a derivative of the C-130B. Illustrated is the second aircraft on an early test flight.

It also spawned a number of derivatives that were optimised to undertake other missions, with these accounting for an additional 74 new-build aircraft. The US Coast Guard's HC-130B search-and-rescue platform led the way, with a dozen examples eventually being obtained. Rather more numerous was the KC-130F in-flight refuelling tanker for the US Marine Corps, with a total of 46 built. The US Navy also acquired the 'Herky-bird' at the beginning of the 1960s, receiving seven pure transport C-130Fs for Fleet logistics support, plus a quartet of LC-130F 'ski-birds' to assist in Antarctic exploration operations. Finally, there was a handful of WC-130Bs, these being the first of several sub-types used on weather reconnaissance duties by the US Air Force.

Subsequent modification of standard C-130Bs in the mid-1960s resulted in the appearance of 11 additional WC-130Bs. Modifications for other missions included intelligence gathering as the C-130B-II, satellite capsule recovery as the JC-130B and specialised research tasks as the NC-130B.

Design and manufacture of the first two versions allowed Lockheed to lay a solid foundation, but when production of

Above: LC-130F 148321 of VX-6 makes a JATO take-off from the Antarctic ice. As a result of a JATO bottle breaking loose in December 1971 this aircraft was abandoned, only to be retrieved from its frozen resting-place in December 1986, repaired and returned to service. Below: Sister-ship 148320 suffered a similar mishap in 1975 but was not badly damaged. PHOTO: P J COOPER

the C-130B was winding down in the early 1960s it is doubtful if anyone associated with the Hercules project could have anticipated that it would still be in production now, nor that more than 1,500 examples would be completed of the next two basic derivatives. Since the C-130 can now be seen carrying the insignia of more than 50 different nationalities, there must have been times when it seemed as if the world was beating a path to Marietta and joining the queue to buy the Lockheed product. That queue started to form with the C-130E, but it was with the later C-130H that Lockheed really reaped the benefit of earlier work.

The C-130E was the third basic version to appear and was to be produced in greater numbers than the C-130A and C-130B combined, with just under 500 examples of all sub-types eventually being completed between 1961 and 1974. About a fifth of those were for export, with overseas customers including Australia, Brazil, Canada, Iran and Turkey. It was also built in large numbers for the Military Air Transport Service (MATS) which was desperate to obtain modern turbine-powered equipment to replace old and obsolescent piston-engined types such as the Douglas C-118 Liftmaster.

Considerable attention was paid to giving the C-130E longer 'legs' so that it could legitimately claim ocean-spanning range with a worthwhile payload. Structural strengthening resulted in maximum take-off weight rising to 155,000lb, although it could be increased still further to 175,000lb by reducing the load factor from 2.5g to 2.25g. At the same time, much larger 1,360 US gall external fuel tanks were added, these being located between the engines, rather than outboard as on the C-130A. Powerplant and propeller installation remained unchanged from that of the C-130B.

The result of these alterations was to boost maximum payload capacity to 45,000lb, which represented a handsome increase over the 35-36,000lb achieved by the two earlier models. As for range benefits, the C-130E was able to airlift

Approximately one-fifth of the C-130E production was sold to overseas air arms. Above: *Canada was already an operator of C-130Bs when it took delivery of the first of 24 C-130Es in December 1964.* Below left: *Argentina received three aircraft serialled TC-61 to TC-63.* Below right: *One of the Turkish Air Force's eight C-130Es.*

20,000lb of cargo some 4,700 miles, while the C-130A could only cover 3,350 miles with a 21,500lb payload.

Production was launched at the beginning of the 1960s, with the first example making its maiden flight on 15 August 1961. A short spell of testing ensued, before deliveries to operational units of TAC and MATS commenced in the spring of 1962. As far as export sales are concerned, the initial customer was Turkey which accepted four aircraft between September and November 1964, with Canada receiving the first of 24 in December of that year.

By coincidence, the C-130H made its début at around the same time, with the basic transport flying for the first time on 19 November 1964, less than two weeks before the HC-130H rescue derivative for the USAF. However, the C-130H was to be a slow starter and less than a dozen pure transport examples were actually delivered (to New Zealand and Norway) during the remainder of the decade, along with 66 broadly similar C-130K Hercules C1s completed for the Royal Air Force between October 1966 and May 1968. Ultimately, though, production of the newest model and a veritable host of derivatives went on to far exceed that of the 'E – indeed, manufacture of the C-130H family accounts for almost half the total number of Hercules aircraft built to date.

At the outset, the C-130H differed from the C-130E in just a few ways. More powerful Allison T56-A-15 engines, rated at 4,508-eshp, were adopted as standard. In addition, it also embodied a redesigned, stronger wing box assembly and an improved braking system. However, during the course of a production run that spans 30 years, many other refinements have since been incorporated and the contemporary C-130H is vastly superior to early aircraft in so far as the avionics suite is concerned, while attention has also been paid to such details as cooling systems.

In the beginning, the standard transport model was supplied only to export customers and it was not until relatively late in the day that the US Air Force decided to acquire the C-130H. Even then, it chose not to invest heavily, taking delivery of just 68 between June 1974 and May 1977 for service with front-line units. All subsequent purchases have been destined for operation with second-line elements of the Air Force Reserve and Air National Guard. This process began with a contract for eight aircraft in the late

Above: *The Royal New Zealand Air Force sent one of its five C-130Hs to Finningley for the Queen's Silver Jubilee Review of the Royal Air Force.* Below: *One of Norway's six C-130Hs based at Gardermoen with 335 Skvadron.* PHOTOS: PETER R MARCH

1970s and subsequent re-orders have raised the number obtained for these organisations to around 200.

As for variations on the C-130E and C-130H themes, these are quite literally bewildering in their diversity. It has been adapted for maritime patrol duties. It has been used as a communications relay platform between US command authorities and ballistic missile-armed submarines lurking deep in the world's oceans. It has been reconfigured to perform electronic countermeasures and psychological warfare tasks. It has been fitted out to undertake covert

City of Ardmore, ***the first C-130A to go on operational duty with the USAF, was in service with the 928th Tactical Airlift Group at Chicago O'Hare at the time of the Hercules' 25th anniversary and*** (below) ***the meet that was held at RAF Greenham Common in 1979.*** PHOTO: PETER R MARCH

operations. It has been modified to serve as a flying hospital – as a gunship – as a bomber – as a weather reconnaissance tool – as a drone launcher – as an airborne command post – as an early warning platform – and even as a VIP transport.

It has been stretched. It has had all kinds of appendages bolted or hung on it. It has endured innumerable weird and wonderful modifications. In the process, it has learnt to accept all manner of indignities with the minimum of fuss, while steadily building a reputation for rock-solid dependability in all kinds of situations. And it is that which is perhaps the greatest of all its many accomplishments.

As for the very first aircraft to be delivered all those years ago, readers might like to know that C-130A 55-0023 went on to enjoy a long and productive career with the Air Force. Like many of its kin, it saw extensive combat action in Vietnam and was in fact damaged by ground fire in March 1968 while serving with the 374th Tactical Airlift Wing. Following repair, it spent time as an NC-130A before reverting to transport configuration for further service with the Air National Guard and Air Force Reserve. Eventually, old age finally caught up with this veteran, but some alert individuals with an eye to history made sure that the one-time *City of Ardmore* was spared the indignity of the cutter's torch. As a result, it now sits in dignified retirement as part of the museum collection at Dyess AFB, Texas.

INTO BATTLE

Although the requirement that ultimately resulted in development and deployment of the Hercules arose out of experience gained during the course of the Korean War, Lockheed's airlifter arrived on the scene about a year after the ceasefire came into effect and was thus too late to play any part in that conflict. Almost exactly a decade later, when the USA again became embroiled in combat in South-East Asia, a very different picture prevailed, for the C-130 was now firmly entrenched in service – and was to undertake a number of vital tasks throughout the bloody and violent conflict that was the Vietnam War.

Some of those tasks were glamorous and attracted considerable publicity. Some were more mundane and were accomplished with little fanfare. Irrespective of that, all had their share of hazards. Since they tended to go in harm's way most often, few would argue that the gunships generally faced the greatest danger, but they were at least able to bring their own weapons to bear against an often unseen enemy.

Transport crews – the much maligned and sorely underrated 'trash and ass haulers' – had no such comfort and sometimes paid a heavy price. A high proportion of the 50 or so examples of the Hercules that were destroyed in the theatre of war between 1965 and 1972 were conventional airlift-dedicated machines.

To do full justice to the part that was played by the Hercules during the Vietnam War really requires an entire book to itself and this volume can do little more than provide an insight into some of the many and diverse missions that were undertaken.

As it has done throughout the type's long and distinguished career, airlift formed the staple diet of the Hercules community during more than eight years of conflict. That involvement essentially began in the spring of 1965, following President Johnson's decision to deploy ground units in-country, when a number of aircraft were tasked to assist in the movement of troops and equipment from the US base at Okinawa to South Vietnam.

Subsequently, as the war effort expanded, so did the extent to which the Hercules supported it, with suitably modified variants undertaking such diverse missions as command and control, rescue and recovery, air refuelling, weather reconnaissance, armed interdiction and even bombing.

Despite the fact that transport-dedicated versions of the Hercules were ever-present in South Vietnam from the spring of 1965 onwards, it should be noted that, unlike the C-123 Providers and C-7 Caribous, none were permanently stationed in-country. Instead, aircraft and crews rotated in and out from home bases situated in the Pacific Air Forces (PacAF) region, such as Naha, Okinawa; Tachikawa, Japan; Mactan and Clark in the Philippines and Ching Chuan Kang, Taiwan.

Normally, each spell of rotational duty lasted for a week or two and initially involved resources drawn from PacAF's own four squadrons, augmented by four Tactical Air Command (TAC) squadrons deployed from stateside bases for 90-day tours of temporary duty (TDY) in the Pacific theatre of operations.

With the build-up of the US presence in the south, the size of PacAF's C-130 force also increased, rising to 12 permanently assigned squadrons by the summer of 1966 and peaking at 15 in the first few months of 1968, with three deployed TAC squadrons on TDY tours. Over the same period, the number of aircraft active on rotation in South Vietnam also rose, from barely a handful in the early part of 1965 to 15 by the summer of that year and on to 32 by year-end. It eventually mushroomed to almost 100 aircraft in February 1968.

Management of this fleet was undertaken by the Common Service Airlift System (CSAS) and its subordinate Airlift Control Center (ALCC) at Tan Son Nhut. The latter organisation was responsible for flight scheduling and controlling daily missions. While it may have been one of the most valuable resources, the Hercules was far from the only airlift asset, for the ALCC also managed types such as the C-7 Caribou and C-123 Provider. In South Vietnam, the most significant and almost certainly the busiest of the Hercules detachments was that at Cam Ranh Bay. This was one of the major aerial port facilities in South Vietnam and hosted some 51 Hercules (23 C-130As and 28 C-130Es) when at its peak in the early part of 1968.

However, that was only part of the overall picture, for other detachments existed: Tan Son Nhut (27 C-130Bs), Tuy Hoa (10 C-130Es) and Nha Trang (8 C-130Es). Between them, these 96 aircraft accumulated somewhere in the region of 14,000 in-country airlift sorties per month, typically carrying around 170,000 passengers and delivering slightly over 60,000 tons of cargo. It was, by any yardstick, an impressive and ambitious undertaking, but the contribution made by the C-130 was only part of the whole picture, since many landing strips were useable only by the C-7 or C-123.

While there may have been places where even the trusty 'Herky-bird' could not go, there can be no doubt that it was

Paratroopers wait to board Tactical Air Command C-130s before transferring to Vietnam.

A TAC C-130B prepares to depart after unloading supplies.

the transport of choice in a lot of difficult situations. Few places were 'hairier' than Khe Sanh in the first four months of 1968 when the 6,000-strong beleaguered Marine garrison was entirely dependent upon tactical transport aircraft. Naturally, the C-130 figured prominently in the resupply effort, with aircraft from both the Air Force and Marine Corps being heavily involved.

Although hailed at the time as a victory, Khe Sanh might best be described as representing a watershed in the war. Certainly, in the post Khe Sanh era, public opinion began to swing ever more vehemently against the fighting, although it was to be another five years before the USA was able to disengage from the nightmare that was Vietnam. In the early part of 1968 such considerations were of little concern to the defenders of Khe Sanh and it is doubtful if many of the aircrew tasked with resupply missions gave them much thought either. They had other far more urgent matters to occupy their minds.

Even allowing for the fact that the US was in the happy position of enjoying air supremacy, resupply of forces on the ground at Khe Sanh was never easy. Weather conditions were seldom favourable and sometimes absolutely foul, often necessitating the use of ground-controlled radar-directed approaches to the drop zones. Then there was the necessity to run the gauntlet of enemy fire, which was often intense though not always accurate.

On good days, it was possible to use the runway, but normal approach procedure was frequently abandoned in favour of the celebrated 'Khe Sanh approach' whereby inbound transports stayed high for as long as they could before nosing over into a steep dive and flaring out to land at the last possible moment. It was not so much a landing as an arrival and while it may not have offered much protection against anti-aircraft artillery pieces, it was a reasonably effective countermeasure against lighter weapons. On bad days – and there were plenty of those – the strip was closed and aerial drops of cargo delivery had to be used, for, like the US mail, the supplies had to get through.

All sorts of procedures were utilised to ensure that the defenders were able to withstand the siege, with the C-130

The Hercules' short-field performance was invaluable in Vietnam in enabling troops to be placed as close to the front-line as possible.

being responsible for the lion's share of the USAF effort which entailed some 1,128 missions between 21 January and 8 April. In total, those missions were responsible for delivering 12,430 tons of cargo to the base. This might not sound like a great deal in the context of the war as a whole but there can be no doubt that it was vital for the Marine defenders.

Overall, the C-130 was responsible for 74% of those missions, with the C-123 completing 24% and the C-7 just one per cent. However, when it comes to considering what those missions achieved, the value of the C-130 comes into even sharper focus. While it may have accounted for only three-quarters of them, it was actually responsible for delivering 92% of the total tonnage airlifted to Khe Sanh.

For obvious reasons, the most desirable method of resupply was simply to land and offload, if only because this ensured that the cargo reached those who needed it. The C-130 completed 273 such deliveries, depositing 3,558 tons of cargo, as compared with 739 tons dropped off by 179 C-123 landings and just 13 tons by eight C-7 landings. Unfortunately, the situation at Khe Sanh meant that landing and offloading was often not possible and other methods had to be employed.

When studying these, even more marked disparities in performance are apparent. Looking first at the Hercules contribution, when using a mixture of containerised delivery drops and both ground proximity and low altitude parachute extraction systems, the C-130 flew in another 7,826 tons in 576 missions, while the C-123 contribution was 294 tons in 105 drops. A simple arithmetical calculation will confirm that the C-130 was just over six times more productive than the C-123.

Khe Sanh was probably the most visible and arguably the best publicised operation undertaken by airlift-dedicated resources during the war, but there were many other missions involving the full range of the C-130's potential. Airdropping paratroops directly on to the field of battle and then keeping them supplied with equipment and ammunition; airlifting combat forces from place to place in support of Army offensive operations; humdrum but necessary cargo hauling tasks. The Herky-bird did it all – and more.

In addition to the pure transport role for which it was designed and at which it excelled, the Hercules was employed for many other missions during the course of the war in Vietnam and it is a fitting tribute to the type's adaptability that it proved conspicuously successful in most of them. Amongst the most unusual tasks were those that required it to be pressed into service as a 'bomber', such as the *Commando Vault* and *Carolina Moon* operations.

The latter was a particularly ingenious but ultimately ineffective attempt to bring down the Thanh Hoa bridge. Also known as the 'Dragon's Jaw', the bridge carried road and rail traffic across the Song Ma river and was of great strategic and symbolic importance to the North Vietnamese. It lay well inside enemy territory and had been a frequently visited target in *Route Pack IV* since the earliest days of the *Rolling Thunder* bombing campaign. Despite achieving some success in temporarily preventing its use, the steel and concrete structure seemed impervious to US bombing and had thus far resisted virtually everything that had been thrown at it by Navy and Air Force strike aircraft.

In the autumn of 1965, however, personnel of the Armament Development Laboratory at Eglin AFB, Florida conceived the idea of mass-focusing the energy of certain high explosive materials to produce a new weapon. Subsequent testing proved that this was a valid concept and one that possessed considerable potential for use against bridges. That was the good news. The bad news was that the resulting bomb was a large device, weighing approximately 5,000lb and measuring some eight feet in diameter with a thickness of about 30 inches. Clearly, such a device was unsuited for use with tactical fighters, but it did not take long for some bright individual to realise it could be carried and delivered by a cargo aircraft such as the Hercules.

News of the weapon's development and potential soon filtered through to higher command echelons in Saigon and serious consideration began to be given to the idea of employing it against the Thanh Hoa bridge. However, since the bridge was extremely well defended by anti-aircraft artillery and automatic weapons, it was fairly obvious that sending a lumbering C-130 directly to the target was likely to end in grief. An alternative approach had to be found and after a certain amount of head-scratching, someone came up with a very cunning plan. Essentially, this envisaged dropping a number of mass-focus weapons up-stream from the bridge, allowing them to travel down river and then be automatically detonated by metal-sensing devices as they floated under the bridge.

Before that could happen, a number of technical difficulties had to be resolved. These included extraction of the weapons from the cargo hold of the C-130, deployment

A C-130A performs a LAPES drop in Vietnam. PHOTO: ROBERT J ELLISON

of parachutes used to lower the large devices into the water and ensuring that they could be delivered with sufficient precision. Those and other obstacles were ultimately resolved and preparations then turned to training for the attack. This was also undertaken at Eglin with the assistance of personnel from the Tactical Air Warfare Center. It involved two C-130s and two crews (possibly drawn from the 61st Troop Carrier Squadron), one led by Major Richard Remers and the other by Major Thomas Case.

By the spring of 1966, they were considered ready to attempt the audacious mission and duly deployed to Da Nang, South Vietnam on 15 May. With them went a total of 10 weapons, sufficient for two attacks, although it was hoped that only one sortie would be necessary. During the period immediately preceding the attack, it became evident that the defences in the vicinity of the bridge had been augmented, but it was decided to press on with the mission which was scheduled to take place on 30 May. The first attack would be made by Remers and his crew, with the Case crew ready to attempt a second raid in the event of failure.

Shortly after midnight, the lone C-130 departed from Da Nang and headed out over the sea, staying at an altitude of about 100ft so as to avoid detection by hostile radars. Other aircraft were also about, with a pair of F-4Cs from the 8th Tactical Fighter Wing at Ubon, Thailand being tasked to carry out a diversionary attack to the south of Thanh Hoa, while an EB-66 jamming platform would be orbiting nearby to electronically mask the approach of the C-130 'bomber'.

The transit proved uneventful and less than an hour after getting airborne the Hercules was over hostile territory, threading its way towards the bridge. Two possible drop zones had been identified, at distances of two miles and one mile from the bridge, with the decision as to which to use being left to the discretion of the crew.

Shortly before reaching the first of the two chosen release points, Remers climbed to the drop altitude of about 400ft and decelerated, opening the rear doors in readiness for weapons release. Thus far, there was no evidence of hostile action and Remers therefore chose to continue to the second drop zone, so as to deposit the weapons much closer to the bridge.

A few seconds after reaching that decision, it became apparent that he had perhaps made an unwise choice, for intense automatic weapon and AAA fire erupted skywards, but Remers now had little option but to continue with the attack. Good fortune stayed with the C-130 and its crew, for the ground fire was poorly directed and posed little threat. A few anxious moments later, all five weapons were gone and the Hercules was running for the sanctuary of the Tonkin Gulf and a safe landing at Da Nang, where the crew waited eagerly for damage assessment.

Reconnaissance aircraft were active at first light and study of the resultant imagery must have been a crushing blow, for it revealed no evidence of damage and no sign of any weapons in the river. It was therefore decided that Major Case would make a second attack on the next night, using basically the same plan with minor modifications to timing and routing. As before, a diversionary attack was to be mounted by two F-4Cs from Ubon.

So it was that C-130E 64-0511 took off from Da Nang soon after 0100 hours and turned northward over the sea. That was the last positive sighting of it, for the second attack went tragically wrong. The demise of the Hercules may have been witnessed by one of the F-4s, since its crew reported observing anti-aircraft gunfire and a ground flash near the bridge just before the time scheduled for the attack, which would seem to indicate that the Hercules was shot down. If that was not bad enough, one of the Phantoms was also lost with its crew. Subsequent reconnaissance of the area around the bridge revealed no evidence of damage or aircraft wreckage and a major search-and-rescue effort also proved fruitless.

A few days after the ill-fated second attempt, the remaining *Carolina Moon* assets were returned to the USA, but an interesting post-script emerged later during the interrogation of a captured North Vietnamese patrol boat crew member. While being questioned, he mentioned an incident in which US aircraft dropped mines in the river close to the Thanh Hoa bridge, informing his captors that four of the devices had detonated successfully but had caused little material damage. It is conceivable that these were the weapons used in the first attack.

As for the bridge, it remained standing despite further determined efforts by US pilots during the rest of the *Rolling Thunder* campaign. It was then spared by President Johnson's 1968 bombing halt and continued in use until 13 May 1972, when USAF Phantoms armed with a mixture of 2,000lb and 3,000lb laser-guided bombs finally succeeded in demolishing a span and putting it out of action.

While *Carolina Moon* may have been short-lived, that was certainly not true of *Commando Vault*, the other operation that entailed use of the C-130 as a bomber. In this case, several hundred sorties were flown over a period spanning approximately five years. While not all of them were overtly offensive in nature, it is fair to say that they were designed to facilitate offensive operations.

The first application of *Commando Vault* came during 1968 and it was initially conceived to create helicopter landing sites in jungle terrain. In a benign situation, this would probably have been accomplished manually, with the aid of chain saws, bulldozers and other equipment. However, the general situation in Vietnam was seldom benign, so another way had to be found. *Commando Vault* was one answer and involved the use of explosives to blast a clear area in the jungle.

While the requirement undoubtedly originated in Vietnam, as was usually the case, the concept was first evaluated in the USA, with personnel from Air Force Systems Command and the US Army co-operating closely to develop ways and means of dropping large bombs from both the C-130 and the Army's CH-54 Tarhe helicopter. Testing of the idea began with the 10,000lb M-121 bomb which was successfully carried and dropped by both types as a prelude to operational employment with effect from the autumn of 1968.

Early drops in Vietnam were undertaken as part of a continuing evaluation and involved both the C-130 and CH-54, with the Hercules being flown by a crew from the 463rd Tactical Airlift Wing. In the case of the C-130, two palletised weapons could be accommodated in the hold, with delivery invariably being accomplished by means of parachute extraction. This normally took place at an altitude of around 7,000ft, whereupon stabilising parachutes deployed to lower the weapon to the ground. Approach to the designated release point relied on the assistance of MSQ-77 ground radar sites and a reasonable degree of precision was achieved. As for the effect, a single M-121 was sufficiently powerful to clear an area about 200ft in diameter. It soon became evident that the Hercules was better suited to the task. For a start, it possessed the ability to deliver two weapons in a single mission, but the real advantage lay in range, for it was able to reach any target from a single loading point.

After a hiatus over the winter months, *Commando Vault* was reintroduced in March 1969 and somewhere in the region of 600 weapons were eventually expended before the ceasefire of 1973. About two-thirds of them were of the even more powerful BLU-82 type, which was first employed in Vietnam on 23 March 1970. It was a 15,000lb device which used a similar delivery technique but which featured a 'daisy cutter' fuse extending rod that detonated the weapon at a height of four feet above ground level, thus making optimum use of blast effect. In practice, it was found that the BLU-82 was able to produce a clearing about 260ft in diameter, and it should come as no surprise to learn that it was also used offensively against troop and vehicle concentrations on a number of occasions.

Although the majority of M-121 and BLU-82 bombs were expended in South Vietnam, where they were usually a precursor to assaults by Army airmobile units, some were dropped in Cambodia and Laos, particularly during 1970-71. Responsibility for providing aircrews to deliver these weapons was initially entrusted to the 463rd Tactical Airlift Wing which retained the capability until late in 1971, when it passed to the 374th TAW. Tan Son Nhut appears to have been the primary centre of 'bomber' operations, with both the C-130B and C-130E models being used during the period in question.

The bombs could have been just as easily delivered by almost any transport-configured Hercules and little special skill was required in actually accomplishing a drop. Indeed, any crew with a reasonable degree of proficiency in airdrop technique could probably have done the job, although pilots needed to be alert to counter a pronounced trim change at the instant of release. Two decades later, when about a dozen examples of the BLU-82 were used against Iraqi troop concentrations and for mine clearance during the course of *Desert Storm*, the task of delivery was given to the MC-130Es of Special Operations Command.

Another hazardous operation involved use of the C-130A as a flareship, primarily for interdiction of the Viet Cong infiltration routes through Laos during the period from 1965

A C-130B loads paratroopers in front of a fuel farm.

A lull in activity creates a typical scene – two Hercules await their next duties .

to 1970. Operating in conjunction with strike aircraft, this was one of a number of concepts intended to overcome difficulties faced by the 'fast movers' (jet fighter-bombers) during the hours of darkness.

At the outset, two code names were allocated to the flareship missions, those undertaken over the *Barrel Roll* interdiction area in northern Laos being referred to as *Lamplighter*, while those against targets in the *Steel Tiger* and *Tiger Hound* areas of southern Laos were called *Blind Bat*. Ultimately, the distinction between the separate zones became blurred and all C-130 flareship missions were eventually referred to by the latter title.

Aircraft assigned to this mission were drawn from the C-130A force at Naha, Okinawa. At the time the *Lamplighter* and *Blind Bat* missions began in January 1965, the Naha-based transport elements were controlled by the 6315th Operations Group, although that unit was replaced by the 374th Troop Carrier Wing (later redesignated a Tactical Airlift Wing) in August 1966. In particular, it fell to the subordinate 41st Troop Carrier Squadron to provide the limited number of aircraft involved, although aircrew to man them were actually rotated from all C-130A squadrons within PacAF's area of responsibility for periods of temporary duty that might last as long as six months.

Operations began at Da Nang, South Vietnam in January 1965, only to be relocated to Ubon, Thailand in March 1966, from where they continued unbroken until 15 June 1970. On that date *Blind Bat* was terminated as a result of the development and deployment of newer systems, most notably on the AC-130 which combined much improved detection equipment with an impressive armament array to produce a devastatingly effective 'hunter/killer' capability within a single airframe.

At peak strength, the *Blind Bat* force numbered a dozen crews and six aircraft. Details of the equipment fitted to the C-130As assigned to this task are sketchy, but they are known to have included image-intensifying starlight scopes for monitoring the ground below, as well as automatic flare dispensers to illuminate areas deemed worthy of attention from accompanying fighter-bombers.

Despite the fact that it was now outmoded, *Blind Bat* had nevertheless done sterling work over the intervening period. This is illustrated by the fact that more than 7,500 operational missions were flown and over three-quarters of a million flares were dropped. Regrettably, these activities were not undertaken without cost, for two C-130As were lost with their crews, apparently as a direct result of enemy action.

Hostile fire also resulted in a number of casualties amongst the celebrated 'gunship' force and no survey of the role of the Hercules in South-East Asia would be complete without some mention of the work performed by these much-modified machines between September 1967, when the prototype conversion was deployed to the war zone for operational evaluation, and 1973, when direct US involvement came to an end.

Even as the first Douglas FC-47 (later AC-47) gunships

were undergoing operational evaluation in Vietnam in early 1965, consideration was being given to development and deployment of a follow-on with superior performance, payload and weaponry. This ultimately led directly to Project *Gunboat* which came into being in mid-1966. Further studies of the concept were undertaken during the summer and autumn of that year and in November personnel associated with the project recommended that the C-130 seemed to be the most suitable candidate for the gunship role.

Money to fund a prototype conversion was soon made available and work on modifying an early production C-130A (54-1626) got under way at Wright-Patterson AFB, Ohio at the beginning of April 1967. The armament package consisted of four 7.62mm mini-guns and four 20mm M-61 cannons, mounted in pairs fore and aft of the wing and firing to port. Other equipment included a Starlight scope image-intensifying device, side-looking radar and a computerised fire-control system linking weaponry and sensors.

In modified form – and now known as *Gunship II* rather than *Gunboat* – the prototype conversion made its maiden flight on 6 June 1967, thereafter moving almost immediately to Eglin AFB, Florida for the first of a series of live-firing trials. These continued into the autumn and culminated in the decision to send the first AC-130A gunship to Vietnam for combat evaluation.

Movement to the war zone occurred in September 1967 and the AC-130A began operations from Nha Trang, South Vietnam on the 24th. It soon demonstrated superior capability, particularly with regard to the interdiction of enemy lines of communication in both South Vietnam and Laos. After approximately 90 days in the theatre, the AC-130A was flown back to the USA for further modifications and general refurbishment, but it was back in action in early February 1968.

On this occasion, it was at first tasked to operate against the Ho Chi Minh trail in Laos and deployed initially to Ubon, Thailand, which was to be the home of the Hercules gunship force for the remainder of the war. In addition, with effect from mid-June 1968, the gunship prototype transferred to Tan Son Nhut near Saigon. From there, it assisted the so-called 'in-country' war, being used in close air support on a number of occasions and also interdicting road and river traffic. It returned to the USA in November 1968.

In the meantime, it had been decided to bring another seven aircraft to a similar standard and work on these had begun in December 1967. Some delays interfered with progress of the conversion programme but all seven were returned to the Air Force between August and December 1968, in time to permit four to be deployed to Thailand and introduced to combat with the 16th Special Operations Squadron before the year ended. Subsequent developments during the late 1960s and early 1970s saw the acquisition of further gunships with heavier calibre weaponry.

This process began with a second batch of ten AC-130As which featured a pair of 40mm Bofors guns. The final 11 aircraft were based on the C-130E airframe, with the resultant AC-130E *Spectre* being the most heavily armed gunship of all, for it was fitted with a single 105mm howitzer

This C-130A (55-0011) was converted to AC-130A standard in October 1969.

The AC-130A fires its guns. The armament package consisted of four 7.62mm miniguns and four 20mm M-61 cannons.

in place of one of the Bofors guns. In conjunction with revision of armament, sensor systems were also progressively updated and in its final form the AC-130 was a vast improvement over the original *Gunboat* prototype.

In almost five years of war, the role of the AC-130 was primarily orientated towards 'out-country' operations and it soon acquired a reputation for being a truck-killer 'par excellence', operating nightly over Laos in a succession of *Commando Hunt* interdiction campaigns. Most missions were targeted against the infamous Ho Chi Minh trail and vast quantities of ammunition were expended in the ultimately unsuccessful effort to cut off the supplies of men and materiel that routinely flowed south under cover of darkness.

In addition, as war spread throughout South-East Asia, a fair amount of energy (and a lot of ammunition) was directed towards the protection of isolated outposts. These activities saw gunships becoming increasingly active over Laos and Cambodia and eventually expanded to include South Vietnam, particularly in the latter stages of the conflict when North Vietnamese and Viet Cong forces prosecuted the war much more boldly and aggressively. At that point in time, the situation became so desperate that operations were also conducted by day, increasing the pressure and dangers faced by the already hard-pressed gunship force.

Inevitably, there was a price to be paid and a total of six gunships fell victim to hostile fire. The first casualty was sustained in May 1969 when one of the early AC-130As was struck by 37mm gunfire over Laos. Although it remained flyable, it was destroyed when it veered off the runway and burst into flames with the loss of two crew members while attempting an emergency landing at Ubon. Just under a year later, in April 1970, a second AC-130A was shot down over the Ho Chi Minh trail. This time, however, only one crew member survived to be recovered by rescue forces.

No further attrition was experienced for nearly two years, but the final phase of the war was also the most hazardous for the Hercules gunship community. Four aircraft and a number of personnel were lost in a nine-month period during 1972.

By this time, Laos was clearly a veritable hornet's nest of anti-aircraft artillery and three of the losses sustained in 1972 occurred there, these involving an AC-130A near Tchepone in late March; an AC-130E at the end of March and another AC-130A near Pakse just before Christmas. In addition, during June, another AC-130A went down over the A Shau valley in South Vietnam after being struck by an SA-7 heat-seeking surface-to-air missile. Despite these tragic events, the gunships continued in action beyond 1972, with the final combat missions being staged over Cambodia shortly before the ceasefire came into effect on 15 August 1973.

During the course of the conflict in South-East Asia, the USA considered and experimented with a succession of often outlandish ideas, several of which involved the Hercules in some capacity or other. Few were successful, but some deserve brief mention, if only to illustrate some of the more bizarre applications to which the Hercules was put.

Perhaps the weirdest was the idea of air-dropping chemicals to destabilise the soil along tracks in the A Shau valley that were frequently used as an infiltration corridor by hostile forces moving south from Laos into Vietnam. It was this idea (appropriately code-named *Commando Lava*) that prompted the US Ambassador to Laos, William H. Sullivan, to advocate the concept of 'making mud, not war' and it was duly put into practice during 1967 when 28 C-130 sorties by aircraft from the 374th Tactical Airlift Wing resulted in 120 tons of chemical compound being scattered throughout the area in question.

Delivery was in fact a fairly sporty proposition, requiring the C-130s to drop down to 200ft in unfamiliar terrain and often in the face of hostile fire which scored more than a few hits and probably caused several anxious moments. Fortunately, no aircraft were lost as a result of battle damage, which was probably just as well since subsequent reconnaissance of the trails and tracks that had been treated showed that the mud-making missions were ineffective. Indeed, it appears that they failed to cause any hindrance to the opposition, which was already well-versed in dealing with the monsoon rains. They simply dumped gravel or bamboo matting over the worst affected areas and then pressed on regardless.

Having abandoned attempts to engulf their opponents in a sea of man-made mud, consideration was then given to enveloping them in a sea of flames, for the US next turned to an idea that could in some ways be likened to the contemporary use of civil and military examples of the Hercules as airborne fire-fighters. In this instance, though, the *Banish Beach* operation had fire-raising as its objective, rather than fire-dousing. Essentially, it involved attempts to set fire to the forest canopy in areas where enemy forces were suspected to be present.

This operation took place in the spring and summer of 1968 and eventually required in excess of 200 C-130 sorties, during which drums of fuel were dropped via the rear cargo ramp in groups of four, with smoke grenades attached to serve as an ignition source on impact. While the idea may have had some merit, it appears to have achieved little and diverted precious flying hours away from urgent transport taskings. As a result, further attempts at fire-raising were formally abandoned at the beginning of 1969.

In summing up the part played by the Hercules during the war in South-East Asia, it is perhaps best to describe it as an indispensable tool, for its versatility allowed it to attempt and usually succeed at tasks that could not have been dreamt of by its designers. Be it as bomber or gunship or airborne command post or pure transport, the *Herky-bird* ranged far and wide through the war-torn skies of Vietnam, Laos and Cambodia for the best part of a decade – and was seldom, if ever, found wanting.

Aerial refuelling of HH-3 helicopters was just one of the many tasks the versatile Hercules dealt with in South-East Asia.

AROUND THE WORLD

Following its entry into service with home and overseas-based commands of the US Air Force, the new tactical transport soon began to draw envious glances from other air arms around the world and Lockheed did not have to wait too long to secure the first of many subsequent export orders. This originated from the Antipodes and involved the supply of 12 late production C-130As to the Royal Australian Air Force (RAAF), which went on to place repeat orders for the subsequent C-130E and C-130H variants.

Delivery of the initial batch of aircraft to the RAAF's No 36 Squadron at Richmond, New South Wales got under way in December 1958, almost exactly two years after the USAF accepted its first examples and it is not perhaps widely realised that Australia was just the second operator to acquire the type, being preceded only by Tactical Air Command. For Lockheed, it was an encouraging start, but it is doubtful if even the most optimistic company executive expected the Hercules to find such widespread acceptance, especially in the early days, when export orders were few – and fairly far between.

Indeed, of the 500 aircraft that had emerged from the assembly hall at Marietta by the beginning of 1963, less than a tenth were produced to meet the needs of a handful of export customers and quite a few of those were actually ordered by the USAF for supply to friendly nations under the auspices of the Mutual Defense Aid Program (MDAP). Apart from Australia, other early operators comprised Canada, Indonesia, Iran, Pakistan and South Africa, but the number of aircraft was far from large, with just 28 C-130Bs involved in these contracts.

Development of the improved C-130E brought more success, with close to 100 examples being built for export to three existing customers (Australia, Canada and Iran) and five new ones (Argentina, Brazil, Saudi Arabia, Sweden and Turkey). However, while the C-130E may have been reasonably successful, it was not really until the advent of the next major model in the mid-1960s that the customer base blossomed and the Hercules became a real money-spinner for both Lockheed and the USA.

This was the C-130H, which was originally developed for the export market at about the same time as the USAF's rescue-dedicated HC-130H. Externally, it closely resembled the C-130E, with the major differences relating to the centre wing box assembly and engine installation. The former was redesigned and strengthened for longer life. The C-130H was also considerably more powerful, following selection of the 4,508eshp (flat-rated from 4910eshp) Allison T56-A-15 turboprop. Improvements were made to the air conditioning and pressurisation systems. Provision for rocket-assisted take-off was initially incorporated, but this feature was deleted in 1975. Other changes made during the course of a long production run mainly concern the avionics suite, which has been updated to capitalise on improvements in this field.

Flown for the first time on 19 November 1964, the C-130H got off to a very slow start and only 11 had been built by the start of 1970. Five of them had gone to New Zealand, which was the launch customer, accepting an initial batch of three aircraft to replace the obsolete Handley Page Hastings in

Royal Australian Air Force Hercules fleet includes both C-130E** (left) **and C-130H** (above) **versions. PHOTOS: PETER R MARCH

Above: *The South African Air Force purchased seven C-130Bs in 1962 and all remain in service today.* Below: *The Royal Saudi Air Force has a large fleet of Hercules, including this C-130H.*

1965. The remainder, delivered in 1969, consisted of two more for New Zealand and six for Norway, although it should be noted that the 66 C-130K Hercules C1s delivered to Britain's Royal Air Force in 1967-68 were essentially similar.

With the start of a new decade, however, the C-130H soon supplanted the C-130E as the basic production model and it has also spawned a number of new derivatives over the years. Many were developed specifically for the US armed forces, but some emerged in response to requests from overseas customers.

Foremost among these is the C-130H-30, a stretched version that is some 15 feet longer than the standard 'H' that has found acceptance with more than a dozen air arms around the world. New missions have also arisen, using

The C-130H-30 is a full fifteen feet longer than the standard C-130H, shown well on this Cameroon Air Force aircraft.

suitably modified aircraft such as the C-130H-MP which is configured for maritime surveillance and search-and-rescue duties and the KC-130H tanker. There is even a version outfitted for the transportation of VIPs, this being known as the VC-130H.

Today approximately one-third of the 2,200-plus examples built or on order have been produced for non-US operators. At the time of writing, the C-130H continues to be the principal production model, but the new-technology C-130J is now just around the corner – and seems well set to capitalise upon the solid foundation laid by earlier derivatives. For much of the past 40 years Lockheed has been in the happy position of being the only supplier of the Hercules. However, during the past decade it has begun to face a certain amount of competition from one of its major customers. This has come about as a result of the USAF retiring substantial quantities of redundant C-130As and C-130Bs, with many of these second-hand aircraft being offered for sale at greatly reduced prices. Not surprisingly, they have proved particularly attractive to less wealthy nations. As a direct consequence, several new air arms have recently appeared on the lengthening list of C-130 operators and it seems reasonable to expect others to look at this source of cheap but effective and reliable aircraft in the coming years.

Worldwide use of the Hercules has resulted in it undertaking a multitude of tasks and missions over the years and it is impossible to provide a comprehensive picture of its diverse use and exploits with such a variety of overseas operators. We have taken just two – the Pakistan Air Force and the Israeli Air Force – both of which have made particularly imaginative use of the trusty 'Herk'.

Pakistan was amongst the earliest purchasers of the C-130 and its operational career with this nation's air arm now spans more than three decades, a period which includes two brief but bloody interludes of conflict with the neighbouring state of India. The first examples of the Hercules to wear Pakistan Air Force insignia were four brand-new C-130Bs delivered under the terms of the Military Assistance Program (MAP) in 1963. These were very soon augmented in No 6 Squadron's line-up by a couple of former TAC aircraft. In later years several more C-130Bs were obtained from the USA and Iran, along with two former Pakistan International Airlines L-100s and five ex Iranian C-130Es.

The Pakistan Air Force (PAF) aircraft were put to good use more or less from the outset and there is no doubt that they represented a huge improvement over the lumbering piston-powered Bristol 170 Freighters previously operated by No 6 Squadron. Paratroop and air-drop missions in conjunction with the Army formed a major part of the squadron's day-to-day work, as did routine cargo-hauling tasks, which frequently entailed the resupply of remote outposts in Kashmir and North-East Pakistan. Missions to the latter area required the C-130 crews to negotiate the Karakoram mountain range. Far from being a joy-ride in the best of weather conditions, it could be decidedly unhealthy for aviators when the weather took a turn for the worst, since the region was notorious in possessing more than its fair share of 'rock-filled clouds' waiting to snare the unwary.

Originally delivered to Iran under the Military Assistance Program, this C-130B (23490) was sold to the Pakistan Air Force in 1967 and remained in service until 1969.

The first 18 months or so of PAF service passed off uneventfully, but 1965 was to be a quite momentous year for No 6 Squadron and its precious few C-130Bs. One notable highlight came in March when all six were involved in the Pakistan Day commemorative flypast over Rawalpindi, but the squadron suffered a major setback in August when one of the C-130Bs was destroyed, just a matter of weeks before the outbreak of the first major period of hostilities with India.

For the Hercules force, the war of 1965 was to prove very challenging, although they had been on something approaching a war footing for several months, in the face of increasingly hostile noises emanating from India. To some extent, this had made life much more difficult, especially with regard to keeping supply lines open between West and East Pakistan, following India's decision to ban overflights of its territory. Henceforth, the C-130s had to go the long way round, flying down the Arabian Sea, skirting Sri Lanka and then heading up across the Bay of Bengal to landfall in what is now Bangladesh.

In addition, from July onwards, No 6 was kept busy ferrying stocks of supplies to Skardu and Gilgit, way up in the North-East of the country. These sorties were undertaken during daylight hours, but squadron personnel were not slow to recognise that the build-up was probably a precursor to serious trouble and that daylight missions might soon become impossible. Accordingly, they began to prepare new mission procedures that would allow them to undertake air-drop sorties by night. The C-130's own weather radar was a vital tool in accomplishing this successfully, but very precise navigation was also essential, as was a complete mastery of instrument flying procedures.

As was the case on a number of occasions before and after the 1965 war, Kashmir was a particular bone of contention between India and Pakistan, especially during the lead-in to full scale conflict. In mid-August, the possibility of war came a stage nearer when Indian troops sealed off the region in order to halt further infiltration by Mujahid forces. Within a very short time, the first requests for supplies to be air-dropped were received by the PAF, with No 6 Squadron professing itself ready and eager to comply to the best of its ability. That was to become quite a challenge for the squadron but it was not put to the test right away, since over a week was to pass before Pakistan's President Ayub Khan authorised the first drop mission.

This was eventually staged on 23 August and was ultimately successful, although the crew experienced some moments of high anxiety during the critical drop phase. Despite that, a 28,000lb load of weapons, ammunition and food was deposited within half-a-mile of the designated drop zone at the second attempt, after storm clouds and severe turbulence resulted in the C-130's speed falling below 100kt during the final stages of the first run.

That was uncomfortably close to the stall, but the situation was not helped by the fact that the aircraft was operating below the mountain tops and the possibility of flying into one of them was ever-present. What made matters even worse was that the crew were flying in near-blind conditions and had to contend with the risk of the radar picture 'toppling' in the event of turbulence being encountered while manoeuvring to reposition for a second attempt. In the event, as already noted, a mixture of skilful flying and good fortune allowed them to make a second approach and the load was successfully despatched more or less right on target.

Yet more exciting adventures were to follow within a month of that hair-raising sortie amongst the mountains, for the scarcely-veiled hostility between Pakistan and India erupted into full-scale warfare on 6 September 1965. Even though the war was short, ending in a ceasefire on 23 September, the Hercules aircraft and crews of No 6 Squadron certainly were not relegated to the role of bystanders – and nor were they content to let others do the fighting, being very much in the thick of things more or less from the outset.

Most of the work allotted to No 6 Squadron was logistical in nature, involving the movement of all sorts of cargo between the various PAF air bases. However, two particular tasks merit closer examination, since they resulted in the C-130s engaging in offensive operations of very different kinds. The first involved air-dropping groups of Army Special Services Group (SSG) commandos well inside Indian territory but turned out to be something of a fiasco, although the C-130 crews involved performed almost faultlessly and cannot be held at all responsible for the failure.

The mission itself was undertaken in the early hours of 7 September and required the services of three C-130Bs, each of which simultaneously dropped a team of 60 paratroops in the vicinity of the major Indian Air Force bases at Adampur, Halwara and Pathankot. The objective was to penetrate the defences at each base and wreak as much havoc as possible before withdrawing.

Unfortunately, since it was viewed as a 'sensitive' force, the SSG tended to work in a vacuum, with planning activity being conducted in isolation from other military echelons. It was in many ways a classic instance of 'need to know' secrecy being taken to extremes and the paratroops committed to action were ill-prepared for the job at hand, being inadequately briefed and, to a lesser extent, insufficiently equipped. About the only thing they were not lacking was courage.

After a couple of delays, the three aircraft involved finally left Peshawar at about midnight, with the drops scheduled for 0210hr on 7 September. Proceeding independently at low level so as to cut the possibility of detection by radar, the C-130Bs succeeded in dropping their respective loads of troops in the designated areas, about two miles from the airfield target complexes. This was felt to be sufficiently far away to allow the commandos to regroup without hindrance, as well as sufficiently close to let them reach their objective as quickly as possible.

As it transpired, unanticipated difficulties soon became evident. Only the Adampur force managed to join up and operate as a concerted entity, but it was able to achieve little. At Halwara and Pathankot, it was a very different story altogether, with the troops coalescing into several small but separate groups, which were unable to bring much firepower to bear. Worse still, the defences were quickly alerted to the presence of enemy forces and the Pakistani soldiers were soon being hunted down by a mixture of Indian Army troops, local police and civilians.

In the hours and days that followed, many of the Pakistani soldiers were killed. Indeed, only a few succeeded in making good their escape from an operation that began in hope and optimism, only to degenerate into a bloody shambles which achieved little of military significance. About the only consoling factor was that their presence caused considerable

Photographed at Chaklala where it serves with No 6 Squadron, this C-130B (58739) was purchased from the United States Air Force in 1981. PHOTO: LINDSAY PEACOCK

Another purchase from Iran was this C-130E (64312), also serving with 6 Squadron at Chaklala. PHOTO: LINDSAY PEACOCK

panic amongst the local civil and military authorities – and prompted the Indian Air Force to temporarily close one of the bases in question.

Even as the ill-fated commando operation was going ahead, an enterprising individual at Chaklala was pushing hard to obtain clearance for a much more imaginative use of No 6 Squadron's talents. This was the station commander, Group Captain Eric Hall, who had already given serious consideration to the idea of adapting the C-130 as a makeshift bomber and now advocated its use on cross-border raids. Hall had earlier been associated with Pakistani use of the Bristol 170 in similar fashion, although the C-130 weapons-release technique was quite different, being fundamentally nothing more than a variation of normal air drop procedure in which bomb-laden cradles were ejected from the rear ramp. Once clear of the aircraft, separation from the cradles would result in the weapons falling individually to the ground.

Hall's preliminary work on this imaginative idea had actually progressed as far as having some cradles and pallets prepared and little time was wasted in devising an operational procedure once the PAF Commander-in-Chief approved the idea. First, it was necessary to test the concept. Wing Commander Zahid Butt, the CO of No 35 (Transport) Wing, undertook a short series of trials on 9-10 September. Sonmiani range was the location used for tests, in which a number of 1,000lb bombs were successfully dropped.

Since it was obviously undesirable to stay around in the vicinity of a target for any longer than absolutely necessary, serious thought was also directed towards finding ways and means of achieving greater drop speeds with the C-130. Eventually, it was found that removal of the rear ramp door allowed safe weapons release at 280kt, which represented a significant increase over the normal maximum airdrop speed of 150kt. Having demonstrated the idea was practical, two C-130Bs were rapidly reconfigured and operational planning forged ahead.

The target for the first mission was a bridge at Kathua, 10 miles to the east of the base at Pathankot and Wing Commander Butt was the pilot in command. His original plan was to approach and bomb the target at low level, so as to reduce the risk of interception by Indian fighters, but operations staff further up the chain of command intervened with the edict that bombing must take place from 8,000ft, which would put the C-130 well above light anti-aircraft artillery fire.

Butt protested vigorously that this would necessitate beginning the climb to drop height some 23 miles from the target, which would place him, his crew and his aircraft at greater risk of running into hostile fighters. In addition, it would materially affect bombing accuracy, but his objections failed to convince his superiors and he had little option but to go ahead with the mission using the revised tactics.

Early on the morning of 12 September, laden with 18 1,000lb bombs, the C-130B took-off and set course for the Pathankot area, Butt maintaining an altitude of no more than 300ft in order to avoid radar detection. In this, he was apparently quite successful, reaching the time-to-climb point unobserved and thereafter gaining altitude steadily as he continued towards the target. Thus far, the Indian forces showed no sign of being aware of Butt's presence and all went smoothly until less than a minute from weapons release.

Then, with barely 40 seconds to go, Butt caught sight of the navigation lights of another aircraft, but kept his knowledge to himself and concentrated on maintaining a steady course during the remainder of the run-in. Moments later, a brief change of trim alerted him to the fact that the bombs were on the move and this was quickly followed by verbal confirmation of a successful drop from the navigator. By then, Butt had lost visual contact with the other aircraft and immediately notified his colleagues of its presence, requesting the loadmaster to check the C-130's vulnerable six o'clock position through the gap left by removal of the ramp door.

Within seconds, the loadmaster reported that they were being pursued by an aircraft without navigation lights. Butt's first instinct was to descend and take evasive action, but he was prevented from doing that by the possibility of over stressing the Hercules. Instead, he reduced power and hauled back on the control column to cut speed to around 160kt, before initiating a 3g turn. Unable to execute a similar manoeuvre, the hostile aircraft overshot and Butt caught a clear sight of it just in front of and slightly below the Hercules.

For a few seconds, it must have presented a fat target and Butt clearly found this most frustrating, since he later confirmed that he might well have shot it down, had the C-130 been fitted with nose guns. Unfortunately, it was not – and the Indian fighter lived to fight another day.

Meanwhile, the evasive manoeuvring resulted in the Hercules rolling out almost directly above Pathankot air base and it very quickly became the target for a sustained barrage of fire by Indian gunners on the ground below. Fortunately for the Pakistani crew, this was inaccurate, but it did delay their descent for a few minutes until they were clear of the area. Only then did Butt drop back to low level, with the remainder of the mission being an anxious but uneventful time.

Subsequent examination of the aircraft used revealed that it had taken a single hit from a 0.5in bullet in the port wing tip. As for the damage inflicted, the PAF was unable to establish just how successful the mission was, but the psychological effect clearly unsettled the enemy. Indeed, on the next day, some Indian radio stations claimed the PAF was using four-engined Chinese bombers – this, however, was clearly untrue.

More bombing attacks followed, with the C-130 force eventually mounting another 13 sorties from a number of PAF air bases before the ceasefire came into effect. Most of these involved the dropping of 18 thousand-pounders, but further work on the idea did result in the payload rising to a maximum of 22 bombs in the closing stages of the war, with this weapons load being used on three occasions.

Irrespective of payload, a similar procedure was employed for each and every sortie, but the altitude restriction meant that the Hercules bomber was limited to attacks on Indian Army forces within reasonably close proximity to the border. The last of these attacks may also have been one of the most spectacular, for two aircraft were used to simultaneously deposit 20 tons of ordnance on artillery emplacements in the Atari area on 22 September. This was evidently highly successful, with post-attack reconnaissance reporting that more than 40 of the 72 guns had been rendered useless. In addition, substantial quantities of ammunition were also destroyed, with secondary explosions continuing for some time as ordnance 'cooked-off' and detonated.

Two interesting footnotes to the bombing operation are worth mentioning. The first was when Group Captain Hall lined all five C-130Bs up at Chaklala for inspection by senior Indian Air Force commanders not long after the war. In so doing, he successfully refuted Indian claims that several had been shot down during the fighting, although it appears that one Indian An-12 *Cub* was destroyed by an SA-2 *Guideline* missile fired by friendly forces near Delhi after being mistaken for a Hercules.

The second relates to the fact that the PAF was in fact the first to utilise the Hercules as a bomber, pre-empting the USA's *Carolina Moon* attempt to knock-out the Thanh Hoa bridge with mass-focus weapons by several months and the more sustained *Commando Vault* operation by almost three years. Pakistani use of the trusty 'Herk' as a bomber was repeated in December 1971, when it again found itself in violent disagreement with India, this time over the secession of East Pakistan – or Bangladesh as it is now known.

On this occasion, war with India was preceded by civil unrest in East Pakistan and the Dacca-based C-130 detachment was kept busy airlifting troops and civilians until shortly before the war began. During this interlude, No 6 Squadron achieved a remarkable feat when one aircraft evacuated no fewer than 365 people from Sylhet to Dacca in a single sortie. With the onset of hostilities, the C-130 flew several bombing missions, against targets that included the airfields at Jaisalmer and Srinagar. As in 1965, these were accomplished without loss and added further lustre to an already impressive reputation.

Another air arm that has made good use of Lockheed's unique transport is Israel's Defence Force/Air Force (IDF/AF). However, for a nation that has depended so heavily upon the USA as a source of military equipment, it may come as something of a surprise to learn that Israel was a relatively late addition to the list of Hercules operators. In fact, approximately 20 other air forces world-wide got their hands on the C-130 before the IDF/AF, which did not obtain its first examples until shortly before the end of 1971, when it accepted a pair of C-130Hs under the Foreign Military Sales (FMS) programme.

Subsequent FMS deals added another eight straight C-130Hs and a brace of tanker-configured KC-130Hs to the inventory during 1974-76. By then, though, the IDF/AF had more than made up for time lost in transitioning to the Hercules, for it had also received a dozen former USAF C-130Es. Hastily withdrawn from Tactical Air Command units, these formed part of the massive infusion of military hardware that was rushed to the Middle East during and immediately after the 1973 Yom Kippur war in which the Israelis once again found themselves locked in battle with the neighbouring states of Egypt and Syria.

Less than three years later, on 27 June 1976, an Air France Airbus A300 carrying over 200 passengers and crew was hijacked by terrorists shortly after take-off from Athens while on a scheduled flight from Tel Aviv to Paris. Instead of heading for the French capital, the Airbus went first to Benghazi and then headed south to Entebbe in Uganda,

Hercules of the Israeli Defence Force/Air Force have been regular visitors to the UK since they were delivered at the beginning of the 1970s. One visited RAF Greenham Common in 1979 to take part in the C-130 25th Anniversary Meet. PHOTO: PETER R MARCH

where the passengers and crew were ordered at gunpoint into the old airport terminal and told that they were now being held hostage by elements of the Popular Front for the Liberation of Palestine (PFLP). As if that was not bad enough, they soon also realised that Uganda's President Idi Amin had colluded in the hijack operation and that their guards included soldiers of the Ugandan Army.

The stage was now set for a rescue attempt that must surely rank as one of the most audacious military exploits ever – and Lockheed's Hercules was a vital part of the successful execution of Operation *Thunderball* by elements of Israel's armed forces. In fact, some might go as far as to say it was the vital part, for the IDF/AF had no other transport aircraft able to carry both the troops and vehicles necessary if the rescue was to stand any chance of succeeding. In that regard, they were perhaps unwittingly helped by the fact that about 150 of the hostages were freed by the terrorists during the week-long crisis, leaving approximately 90 captives inside the building at Entebbe.

Planning for *Thunderball* was undertaken in great secrecy, even as the Israeli government at first stonewalled and then reluctantly agreed to negotiate with the hostage-takers so as to buy time while military options were explored. Against that background, strenuous efforts were made to obtain up-to-date intelligence from a variety of sources and these soon bore fruit. Nonetheless, it was not until several days into the crisis that the balance shifted in favour of a military operation to free the remainder of the captives.

It was, in every respect, a daunting prospect. Firstly, the rescuers had to be transported 2,400 miles from Israel to Uganda. Secondly, the troops involved in any rescue attempt had to be deposited on the ground with the minimum of noise and fuss, so as not to alert the terrorists to the impending action. Thirdly, the size of that force had to be sufficiently large to allow all military objectives to be accomplished swiftly, but not so large as to make the operation unnecessarily complex. Fourthly, the troops and hostages then had to be flown 2,400 miles back to Israel. Finally, planning and preparation had to be utterly 'leak-proof', since even the vaguest threat of a rescue attempt would have dire consequences for the hostages.

On Saturday 3 July, exactly one week after the hijacking, the Israeli cabinet met to consider the plan presented to them by Chief of the Defence Staff General Mota Gur and voted unanimously to implement Operation *Thunderball*. Within minutes, their decision was passed to the Defence Ministry and at 1530hr a coded message was transmitted to the lead aeroplane, for the force of four aircraft had taken-off some 90 minutes earlier and were even now being escorted by a clutch of F-4 Phantoms as they droned out over the Red Sea.

On board the C-130s were almost 250 commandos and several heavily armed jeeps. Most incongruous of all, though, was the presence of a black Mercedes saloon car. This was embarked simply as a ruse and it was hoped the Ugandan soldiers would mistake it for Idi Amin's personal vehicle, thus giving the assault force a few extra precious seconds in which to do their deadly work.

Transit to the destination at Entebbe passed off more or less uneventfully, with the route that was used taking the formation more or less due south down the Red Sea at low level. In the vicinity of Djibouti, the leading C-130 turned on to a south-westerly heading and began climbing to 20,000ft – behind it, the other three aircraft soon did likewise, using SKE (Station-Keeping Equipment) to maintain the desired separation in an electronic game of 'follow-my-leader'. Ahead lay several more hours of flight across Ethiopia and Kenya, before they would go into action.

Other Israeli aircraft were also active that night. One was a Boeing 707 that was outfitted as a flying hospital, with operating tables and medical staff. This was flown to Nairobi to await the aftermath of the rescue attempt. Another Boeing 707 also had a part to play, but this was configured as an airborne command post and would orbit over Lake Victoria to monitor the approach of the C-130s and jam Entebbe's radar during the critical period of the assault.

Shortly before midnight, using a fictitious African airline call-sign, the pilot of the leading Hercules radioed for landing permission from the Entebbe control tower. Unaware of the deception, this was granted and the C-130 continued its descent, passing low over Lake Victoria and breaking out of the mist with just a matter of seconds to go before touch-down. Inside the hold, the commandos were ready to disembark as soon as the aircraft had come to a halt and lowered its ramp. Moments later, it was down and rolling to a parking spot some distance from the old terminal and hopefully well out of earshot of the terrorists.

Shortly afterwards, the other three aircraft landed in quick succession, one using the same runway as the leader and the other two touching down on the much shorter old runway. Having lowered their ramps to allow the ground force to go into action, all the aircrews could do now was wait.

Within a matter of minutes, it became clear that the assault had been successful. All seven of the terrorists were killed in less than two minutes. As for the poorly trained and ill-equipped Ugandan soldiers, few of them showed much stomach for a fight and many instead chose to melt away into the night, leaving the way clear for Israeli sappers to place explosive charges on Amin's small force of MiG-17 and MiG-21 fighters.

Elsewhere on the airfield, with the situation now more or less under control, no time was wasted in calling up two C-130s to load the hostages. Most of them had survived their ordeal unscathed, but two had sustained fatal injuries in the brief but violent battle and several more had gunshot wounds. Embarkation was completed swiftly and they were immediately flown out, with the first Hercules leaving Entebbe just 40 minutes after the most critical phase of *Thunderball* had begun.

The other three aircraft followed suit in quick succession, at the end of a spectacularly successful operation. The primary objective of freeing the hostages had been achieved and the cost in terms of human life was relatively light, although the force commander died after being struck by a sniper's bullet while overseeing the evacuation of the hostages. Despite that tragic loss, Israel had demonstrated its determination not to surrender to terrorism and Lockheed's Hercules had been crucial in bringing that about.

Four Israeli Hercules similar to the one depicted above took part in the Entebbe rescue.

THE RAF'S *FAT ALBERT*

The first RAF Hercules is handed-over with due ceremony.

On 19 December 1966, resplendent in its original natural-metal factory finish, the first of 66 examples of the C-130K Hercules C1 whistled in to Teversham Airfield, Cambridge after a trans-Atlantic ferry flight that was not without drama. During the crossing, the aircraft concerned (XV177) experienced a near-total electrical failure, but it made it safely to Marshall's engineering and overhaul facility on the outskirts of Cambridge. Here, it received final preparation for delivery to the Royal Air Force, a process that involved the installation of British-manufactured auto-pilots and navigation equipment as well as painting in the two-tone brown and black camouflage scheme specified by the service for all of its new transports.

Acquisition of the Lockheed machine for the RAF came about as a direct result of the government decision in February 1965 to cancel the Hawker-Siddeley HS681 jet-powered tactical transport project. Hot on the heels of that unfortunate event, a study group was set up to consider possible alternatives that might be obtained to replace existing transport aircraft types such as the Handley Page Hastings and Blackburn Beverley. It did not take long for the group to recognise that the Lockheed C-130 was far and away the most suitable candidate and they duly recommended that the Hercules be purchased as soon as possible.

Political and more especially economic considerations did not permit the HC-130H, that was at the time in production for the USAF, to be obtained completely 'off-the-shelf'. Part of the deal that was eventually negotiated with Lockheed specified the use of selected items of British-manufactured equipment, with final fitting-out to be done by Marshall of Cambridge. These items made the finished transport aircraft sufficiently different to merit adoption of a new designation. All 66 aircraft that were ordered were initially designated by the manufacturer as C-130K-C1s.

For the most part those revisions related to avionics equipment but some individuals argued strongly for the replacement of the Allison engines by the Rolls-Royce Tyne. Fortunately, wiser council prevailed and the Hercules was ultimately delivered with the standard T56-A-15 turboprop as installed on the C-130H, thus avoiding any risk of a repetition of the engine-related problems experienced with the Spey-powered Phantoms that were obtained at around the same time.

The first C-130K (XV176) made its maiden flight from Marietta on 19 October 1966. Although it had been the first example to emerge from the assembly hall, XV176 was retained for test flying by the manufacturer for some months – and responsibility for British service acceptance trials fell to the second and third machines (XV177 and XV178). They joined the Aircraft and Armament Experimental Establishment's test fleet at Boscombe Down in February and March 1967 respectively.

Since the design was well-proven and had a decade of service behind it, the trials programme was completed quite

A Hercules from the Aircraft and Armament Experimental Establishment at Boscombe Down demonstrates the Ultra Low-Level Airborne (ULLA) delivery system early in 1970.

swiftly and crew training was soon under way with No 242 Operational Conversion Unit (OCU) at RAF Thorney Island. Building up rapidly to its authorised strength of six aircraft, the OCU functioned as the RAF's 'Hercules University' and began turning out qualified aircrews by the summer of 1967, allowing the first of the Hercules front-line squadrons, No 36, to form at Lyneham in July 1967.

No 36 Squadron began operations on 1 August, and was rapidly followed by No 48 Squadron at RAF Colerne. However, the later unit's permanent home base was to be at Changi, Singapore, with the process of replacing the veteran Hastings getting under way there in October 1967. Back at RAF Lyneham, No 24 Squadron started flying the Hercules in February 1968. As there was then insufficient space at

XV177 was used for training the RAF's new Hercules crews at No 242 Operational Conversion Unit at RAF Thorney Island.
PHOTO: PETER R. MARCH

demanding example in my recollection is drawn from the period in 1979/80 when a Commonwealth Monitoring Force (CMF) was sent to Rhodesia to oversee the end of the civil war and to put in place arrangements that would allow the holding of free elections, and lead to the emergence of an independent Zimbabwe.

The in-theatre air forces for this operation comprised RAF Hercules, RAF Puma helicopters, and Army Air Corps Gazelle helicopters. The task for the Hercules turned out, unexpectedly, to be the initial distribution and subsequent air re-supply of the army forces that would bring about the assembly of the warring factions into specified areas, so that the elections could be held following an effective ceasefire. Initial plans to achieve these objectives by road transport were thwarted when most roads were found to be mined; the problem of distribution thus fell to the air forces. Our task was complicated by the difficulties of persuading the fighting troops out in the field of the peaceful intentions of the CMF aircraft. Guerrilla armies were widely spread throughout a country the size of the United Kingdom and the North Sea combined, and fast, effective communications seemed unlikely. The terrain is very varied, ranging from sharply mountainous areas to flat veldt and it is spread over three distinct plateaus, of which the central plateau is the highest, at some 5000ft above sea level. Inevitably, the geography of the country was unfamiliar to the RAF aircrews, except to the extent that it might be imagined from studying an atlas. Likewise, the threats posed by the civil war were also unknown, as were the types of weapon used by the guerrillas. So it was a perplexing task presented to the aircrews at the start of the operation.

When I flew in to Salisbury (now Harare) with my crew and aircraft in mid-December 1979, we were the first to arrive in theatre, and had very little idea of what lay ahead of us. Nevertheless, we were reasonably confident that whatever the task, we would be able to find some way of doing it; we also had confidence in the reliability and versatility of our aircraft. This view was not shared by the indigenous Rhodesian Air Force, whose veterans suggested that several years of experience would be needed before the RAF could operate efficiently in the local environment. Despite this scepticism, Rhodesian Air Force aircrew were very helpful in providing the best information they had about likely high threat areas, weaponry, and other intelligence.

The Rhodesian aircraft had the advantage of special fitments to counter the widespread threat from infra-red guided surface-to-air missiles (SAMs). We had neither the time nor the facility to make such modifications to the Hercules, which meant that our protection would have to come from devising effective tactics. We were also dismayed to discover that the Hercules had already been used around the country, and that all the Patriotic Front forces would therefore be likely to regard our aircraft as hostile. The only features that identified us as part of the

One of the Hercules used during Operation Agila *(XV304), seen here at Lyneham after its return to the UK.* PHOTO: ANDREW MARCH

CMF were two large white crosses, hurriedly painted in emulsion on either side of the aircraft's nose. Now they would make good aiming points!

We needed to devise our own tactics and put them into operation as soon as possible. The danger appeared to divide itself into two distinct areas: the SAM threat, valid up to 14,000ft above ground level (agl); the threat from other weapons systems, generally limited to 2000ft above ground. The main centres of population – Salisbury, Bulawayo and about four other sizeable towns – were generally free of these threats, so could be climbed above and descended toward with relative impunity. It should therefore be possible to climb or descend above them in a tight spiral, and then to transit at heights in excess of 14,000ft agl. However, we also needed to land at unprotected airstrips all around the country, as well as use air drop zones (DZs), which could be set up virtually anywhere. At the strips and the DZs the aircraft would need to be either on, or very close to the ground. We were unavoidably faced with flying between the towns and the strips/DZs, either at the mercy of SAMs or other weapons.

SAMs are virtually unusable against a low flying target, but small arms and Anti-Aircraft Artillery (AAA) are not; on the other hand, if the aircraft flies very low and reasonably fast, the risk from these weapons is much reduced. If we were to minimise the threat, we had to answer the question: how low and fast could *Fat Albert* (the RAF nickname that so aptly describes the C-130) be flown? Low level flying training in RAF Hercules is normally carried out at 250ft agl, and at a speed of 210kt. Low flying is a specialist skill and requires both training and aptitude to be carried out safely and accurately. Additionally, we already knew that the difference between flying at 500ft above the ground and 250ft above the ground is very noticeable. How much greater would the difference be when flying significantly below 250ft and at much higher speeds?

All of these questions could only be answered by planning and flying an experimental sortie. If we could fly low enough and fast enough we would get home safely; if not, somebody else would have to find an alternative solution. We plotted what we imagined would be a typical trip, flying high between Salisbury and Bulawayo (which is about 300 miles south of Salisbury), then continuing at low level to the south east, and northwards along the eastern border, calling at strips called Gwanda, Rutenga and Mutandahwe before returning to Salisbury. The weather was good, and promised to remain so over the whole area that we intended to circumnavigate. Flight planning involved drawing the route up on the topographical maps that we had been provided with, as well as the ones we had scrounged locally. Both sets turned out to be inaccurate, with badly presented, or even inaccurate, topography, but perhaps more worryingly with a lack of up-to-date obstruction data. At low level the options are seriously reduced when rounding a blind corner to find a 500ft unmarked mast directly ahead. This point was later underlined by one of the other pilots who commented that a lot of the flying was up valleys that he would not normally even think of driving through!

The Hercules' performance made it ideal for operations in Rhodesia. PHOTO: PETER R. MARCH

Members of Operation* Agila *on their return to RAF Lyneham. The white cross of the Hercules has been embellished with mission symbols. Sqn Ldr (now Wg Cdr) Tony Webb (lower left).

Once the routes were drawn up, they were carefully studied so that features might be readily recognised, and to identify lead-in points close to landing strips. This was to be solely a training trip, so there was no payload to worry about, and no air drops to take into account. Out at the aircraft there was little to do besides checklist completion and discussion of the minor technical snags that we were carrying whilst operating away from our home base. We started up and taxied out to the runway.

After take-off we started the spiral climb in a fairly tight orbit, and spent about ten minutes reaching the cruising altitude of 14,000ft above ground, which was actually 19,000ft above sea level. The transit to Bulawayo was uneventful, as was the descending spiral over the town. The interesting part of the trip was about to start. As we set off eastward, I rapidly descended to 250ft, and accelerated to an Indicated Air Speed (IAS) of 270kt, which was about as fast as a Hercules can go without risking damage. IAS, however, can be lower than actual – or True – airspeed, because of the effects of air density; this part of Zimbabwe is 5000ft up, and the real speed across the ground was just under 300kt, or about 340 mph. The impression of speed was a little more obvious, but increased speed alone seemed to make more difference to noise levels than to visual cues.

When we started to descend below 250ft, however, the impression of speed rose dramatically. At this stage many thoughts passed through my mind; first, there was a very real threat from a variety of weapons systems; second, flying this low and fast was a very different experience from routine training; third, the wing span of the C-130 is 132ft 7in, half of which was sticking out every time you banked to turn a corner; fourth, things were happening very fast, and obstacles appeared and were passed in the blink of an eye; fifth, the degree of concentration required was very high, which reduced one's ability to take in additional information. Many other thoughts formed and faded, mainly connected with the newness of the experience. The thrill of it all, and the feeling of achievement which it conveyed easily overrode any anxiety, and the sheer pleasure in manoeuvring such a large aircraft so close to the ground shut out fears of any risks which might be involved. Trees and mounds of stone flew past; progress seemed to involve a continuous series of turns to avoid obstacles. Reminders of the wing span were constantly triggered by noticing that the radar altimeter (which gives a very accurate reading of height above the ground immediately beneath the aircraft) was reading between 50 and 90ft. That meant that unless the aircraft climbed slightly every time a corner was turned there was a good chance of hitting something. On the other hand, keeping low was equally important to survival and the loadmaster (ALM) reported seeing several tracer streams just behind the aircraft – so it was clear that the predicted threat was indeed a reality. Nevertheless, the consuming thrill of the experience overcame all other distractions.

As experience of the terrain was gained, it became clear that there were wide variations; even the flatter areas contained similar looking trees and shrubs which grew to different heights in different regions, a variation that could easily undermine judgement of aircraft height above the ground. The next challenge was to find the first landing strip – Gwanda. At the planning stage we had calculated that a Hercules should be able to slow down from 270kt to landing speed (tactical landing speed is around 100kt, unless the aircraft is very heavy) in a distance of about 12nm. The idea was to close the throttles when about 14nm away, and to select the flaps and undercarriage as the aircraft decelerated through the appropriate speeds.

In this way, the aircraft should arrive at the landing threshold at the right speed, in the right configuration and with power re-applied to hold the speed. The psychological problem of doing this was considerable, since all training and previous experience associated landing with descending, and with having a good visual picture of the landing strip or runway *before* touchdown. However, the new procedure would deprive the pilot of a view of the strip until the last few seconds before actually landing, and would not provide the usual feeling of confidence which a visual analysis gives. Nevertheless, the plot worked, and we arrived at Gwanda at about the planned time, which proved that both it and the aircraft were in the expected place! The landing might not have been the smoothest I had ever made but the aircraft touched down firmly and squarely at the end of the strip, and the combined effect of reverse thrust and powerful brakes brought it to a rapid halt just 1000ft later.

The rest of the trial sortie passed off without significant incident, but provided invaluable practice at very low flying, and how it had to be adapted to changing terrain; it also illustrated that this routine was extremely tiring. Later on, when we were flying almost continuously between dawn and dusk, we found it essential to transfer control between pilots fairly often, and for the non-operating pilot to watch the one flying the aircraft for signs of exhaustion – in addition to reading the maps and all the other tasks of keeping up with the aircraft's progress. The motorway/long distance driving syndrome of severe drowsiness was much in evidence, and could all too easily lead to sudden catastrophe.

The effects of adrenalin changed with frequent use; the sudden shock reaction slowly changed into a semi-permanent heightened awareness. Another effect of spending virtually all one's waking hours in an aircraft, day after day, was to react to the flight deck environment as 'home' and to actually relax in the place where you normally sharpened your attention. These confusing reactions needed to be analysed and allowed for in crew routines. Communications between all crew members were modified in ways which reduced the number of words spoken, but increased the meaning conveyed. Much of this modification was instinctive rather than contrived, and was, I believe, a good example of the wisdom of choosing crews with the widest experience and training for tasks which present the greatest challenges.

The operation in Zimbabwe lasted for over three months, and the Hercules element managed to avoid an accident, although there were a number of near misses. Good fortune played a part in this outcome, and the often fatal convergence of bad luck and bad judgement never occurred. Operation *Agila* provided an outstanding example of the adaptability of the Hercules, with one particular aspect highlighting how rugged and sturdy the aircraft is. Under normal circumstances, hitting a bird in flight is potentially very hazardous and is followed by diversion to the nearest airfield and an inspection of the damage. During *Agila* birdstrikes were such a common experience that they were ignored until the next planned landing, and the damage either left alone or given a temporary repair. To have done otherwise would have been seriously to inhibit the whole operation, but the confidence in the aircraft which this remarkable resilience gave to the crews is a tribute to Lockheed's excellent aeroplane. Other aspects of reliability were underlined by the astonishingly high success rate of the daily programme. Over the whole operation, that involved six aircraft flying four or five trips each day, but only two sorties were lost due to unserviceability. There were, of course, many system failures, but the aircraft's inbuilt redundancy, combined perhaps with the crews' willingness to accept faults, enabled nearly every trip to be completed successfully.

The fine qualities of the Hercules in meeting the challenges of humanitarian aid can be no better illustrated than this account written for *RAF News* by Christopher Yorke-Edwards reporting from Addis Ababa, Ethiopia.

The RAF carried out the first food drop of its famine relief operation in Ethiopia, on Saturday 26 January, some 100 miles north-east of Addis Ababa. It was near to the small town of Rabel on a plateau about 10,000ft above sea level, surrounded by deep ravines and gorges and completely inaccessible by road transport. Neither is it possible to serve the area by an air strip. The Ethiopian Government was concerned that such areas were not being reached by the famine relief operation and it was Assistant Secretary-General of the United Nations, Mr Kurt Jansson, who suggested that air drops might be carried out.

Once the idea was put forward to the RAF, they called on their previous experience of making similar drops to see how it could be adapted for the job in hand. It was clear that the drops were not going to be straightforward. For a start, the altitude of the mountainous regions of Ethiopia meant the Hercules C-130 transport aircraft's performance would be degraded – high temperatures would also aggravate the problem. But perhaps the biggest problem would be to get the grain on the ground without the bags splitting and spilling their life-saving cargo.

A Hercules from RAF Lyneham delivers food in Ethiopia as part of the huge international humanitarian effort.

Two practice drops were tried at Addis Ababa airfield and the RAF in conjunction with an Army team made up of 47 Air Despatch Squadron, Royal Corps of Transport, were then confident they could get the bags down on the ground in one piece. The idea is that up to 20 sacks of grain, each weighing about 110lb are tied to a thick plyboard sheet. The boards and sack are then pushed out of the back of the aircraft, which has to fly at around 50ft and at a ground speed of 140mph miles an hour. Bearing in mind that this speed is close to the minimum at which the aircraft can stay in the air, the fact that its performance is degraded by the altitude anyway, and the unforgiving terrain, it is a very tricky operation which requires the utmost skill by the aircrew.

The first drop of Operation *St Bernard*, as it is known, was carried out by members of 47 Squadron, based at Lyneham. The captain of the aircraft was Flt Lt Jim Norfolk, who is an instructor with the Support Training Wing at Lyneham. As the aircrew brought the aircraft over the dropping zone four members of 47 Air Despatch Squadron, RCT – the fact that the squadrons numbers are the same is coincidence – pushed a total of eight pallets from the back of the aircraft two at a time, in four separate passes.

They fell very close to the target – in fact one drop actually demolished the sheets which marked the spot. If the aircraft performance is degraded at this kind of altitude, then so is that of the human body. With oxygen levels low and each load ejected from the aircraft weighing one and three quarter tons, it was no mean effort, particularly as the crew had already spent many hours loading back at Addis Ababa.

Brute force was not all that was required. The cords attaching the sacks had to break at a pre-determined force, so the sacks successfully separated from the boards on impact. Not only were the bags dropped on target but the initial estimate is that more than 90% of the sacks landed intact. As well as being the first operational airdrop, this mission was by way of a demonstration that it could be done. Many Ethiopian officials and representatives of relief agencies were at the drop zone to witness it. It is estimated that in the area of today's drop 175,000 people are in need of food.

MORE CONFLICT

Even though it is best known for its humanitarian exploits, the C-130 Hercules is no stranger to the hazards of battle. Its use in the Vietnam War is legendary, but combat experience certainly does not end there, for it has seen action with a number of other air arms around the world. Great Britain's Royal Air Force had to wait some 15 years before the Hercules got the chance to show its mettle in combat. That opportunity finally presented itself from 2 April 1982 following Argentina's invasion of the Falkland Islands. Since it constituted the most visible evidence of British intent to retake the islands, the activities of the naval task force that headed south dominated the headlines, but the Hercules also played its part, both during the conflict and in the period that followed, when it single-handedly formed the 'air-bridge' to Port Stanley until a new airport at Mount Pleasant was eventually constructed and opened.

At the outset, the RAF aircraft did not have the 'legs' to operate the long distances across the South Atlantic, but two hurried modification projects soon overcame this shortcoming. The first entailed fitting auxiliary fuel tanks in the cargo holds of a number of C1s in order to boost their range. This inevitably cut down on payload and was far from being the ideal solution. The second was infinitely superior but took more time to accomplish. This involved the addition of in-flight refuelling probes and associated plumbing. The source of the probes was the Vulcan bomber, which was then in process of being retired, and some 16 examples of the Hercules soon carried this invaluable item of equipment. At around the same time, a handful of aircraft were fitted as single-point C1K tankers, but these did not come on the scene until after the war had ended.

Inevitably, much of the work undertaken during Operation *Corporate* concerned the movement of cargo and personnel from the UK to the mid-Atlantic staging base at Ascension Island. However, once probe-equipped aircraft became available in the middle of May, the Hercules was periodically employed to air-drop mail and supplies to elements of the task force in the vicinity of the Falkland Islands.

The first air-refuelled air-drop mission was staged on 16 May by a crew from No 47 Squadron led by Flight Lieutenant Harry Burgoyne. During the course of a sortie that lasted just over 24 hours, they covered approximately 7,000 miles and delivered 1,000lb of stores and eight parachutists to a destination that remains unknown even today, more than 12 years after the event. Even more intriguing are reports that at least two RAF aircraft operated from Punta Arenas in Chile during the war with Argentina and that these machines were

As a result of the Falklands War a number of RAF Hercules C1s were fitted with in-flight refuelling probes removed from obsolete Vulcan bombers. PHOTO: PETER R MARCH

Both sides in the Falklands War made use of the Hercules – Argentina's fleet included KC-130H tankers that were used to refuel their fighters.

given Chilean Air Force insignia to disguise their real origins. As for the nature of the tasks they performed, nothing is known, but they may well have involved the covert insertion of Special Air Service personnel into neighbouring Argentina.

These and other missions all contributed to the RAF Hercules fleet accumulating some 10,000 flying hours in barely six weeks, but they were not the only Hercules that were involved in the conflict. Argentina also operated the C-130 and was equally determined to put its transports to good use. At the time, the Fuerza Aerea Argentina (FAA) possessed about ten aircraft – most were pure transport C-130H models, but there were also a couple of KC-130H tankers that were used to refuel fighter and attack aircraft intent on engaging British forces.

These tanker-configured aircraft generally kept well clear of areas where RN Sea Harriers prowled, but the standard C-130H transports were considerably more adventurous and one was shot down by a Sea Harrier on 1 June. Despite that, resupply missions continued until 13 June, less than 24 hours before the surrender. A total of 31 sorties was made to Port Stanley in order to deliver supplies to the Argentine garrison. Most were accomplished at extremely low level under cover of darkness. Some 400 tons of cargo were flown in, with 264 casualties being evacuated to the mainland. In addition, two air-drop sorties were made to outlying locations.

Argentina also adapted one of its C-130Hs to serve as a 'bomber', although it appears that this achieved little success and inflicted only minor damage on British shipping. One bombing raid is known to have taken place on 29 May, when the fuel-laden 15,000-ton *British-Wye* was the target for a string of eight bombs. Unfortunately for the British crew, one of these weapons found its mark – but disappointingly for the Argentinean crew, it failed to detonate and simply bounced off the ship.

Just over a week later, on 8 June, the Argentine AF tried again. On this occasion an intelligence failure resulted in great embarrassment for the Argentineans, since the ship which came under attack was a US-leased oil tanker which had nothing to do with the conflict. By an extraordinary coincidence, the vessel's name was *Hercules* and it was hit by at least one bomb. As before, this failed to explode, but it did end up lodged deep inside the ship, which was eventually scuttled.

While military operations to recapture or retain the Falkland Islands presented the RAF and FAA with a number of demanding challenges, the amount of effort that was expended pales into insignificance when compared with events that occurred some nine years later, during the ejection of Iraqi forces from Kuwait. Since the C-130 was the premier tactical airlift aircraft with several of the air arms that contributed forces to the Allied coalition, it should come as no surprise to learn that the Hercules was deployed in some strength.

The US contribution was by far the largest, with some 200 C-130s being deployed to several locations across the Gulf area. The lion's share came from the Air Force. Airlift C-130E and C-130H models drawn from a number of first and second-line units recorded close to 12,000 sorties during the *Desert Shield* operation that preceded full-scale combat. During the course of the build-up Military Airlift Command (MAC) established a number of provisional transport units to fulfil in-theatre airlift tasks. The C-130s assigned to these temporary organisations were kept busy moving vast quantities of men and material as more and more US forces poured in.

The pressure increased with the shift into war. One notable operation was the 82nd Airborne Division's move from its staging area to positions near the Kuwait border so

Not surprisingly, the United States Air Force provided the lion's share of Hercules taking part in Operations **Desert Shield** *and* **Desert Storm.** PHOTO: DANIEL J MARCH

as to be ready to take the offensive when the ground war got under way. Such activities frequently involved use of rough desert strips and the C-130's 'go-anywhere' ability proved of considerable value during this phase.

In addition to airlift, several special mission aircraft were also despatched to the Gulf. A handful of AC-130H Hercules Gunships from the 16th Special Operations Squadron provided fire support during *Desert Storm*. Indeed, the only example of a Hercules to be destroyed during the build-up and the war itself was an AC-130H (69-6567). It was shot down with the loss of all 14 crew members by a shoulder-launched surface-to-air missile when it went to the assistance of Marine forces on 31 January. Older 'gunships' also saw combat action. The Air Force Reserve's 711th SOS deployed some AC-130As to Turkey for operation *Proven Force*, which put pressure on enemy troops in the north of Iraq.

Less is known of the activity undertaken by the USAF's MC-130Es, although it appears that about half-a-dozen aircraft from US and European-based units were present. It appears likely that these were used for covert insertion and extraction of Special Forces personnel. They are also reported to have played some part in psychological warfare (psy-war)

The AC-130H Hercules 'gunship' was prominent in the Special Operations Role.

EC-130E(RR) aircraft from the 193rd Special Operations Squadron, Pennsylvania Air National Guard were also used for electronic and communications duties. PHOTO: ANDREW MARCH

operations by scattering leaflets in areas of Iraqi troop concentrations. The Hercules was again used as a makeshift bomber aircraft, with the MC-130E depositing about 10 examples of the 15,000lb BLU-82/B fuel/air explosive weapon along the Kuwait border. Most were expended in order to clear minefields but some may have been aimed at enemy troops.

Various versions of the 'electric' Hercules were also there in limited numbers. The Air National Guard EC-130E(CL) and EC-130E(RR) were used to obtain electronic and communications intelligence as well as for psy-war operations, while regular Air Force EC-130Es undertook the ABCCC (Airborne Battlefield Command, Control and Communications) task. Several EC-130H *Compass Call* aircraft supported strike forces by jamming and disrupting Iraqi radar sites and communications networks. Last, but by no means least, a number of Air Force HC-130N and HC-130P models were available for combat search-and-rescue duties and to refuel MH-53J helicopters engaged on special operations.

A limited number of US Marine Corps Hercules participated in Desert Shield. PHOTO: PETER R MARCH

The French Air Force Hercules fleet from Orléans-Bricy was also operated in the Saudi Arabian desert. PHOTO: PETER R MARCH

The Navy and Marine Corps use of Hercules was smaller and probably numbered no more than 20 aircraft. The former service is known to have used C-130Fs for logistics support and also deployed the EC-130Q which functioned in a communications relay role. As for the Marines, they established tanker task forces with an assortment of KC-130Fs, KC-130Rs and KC-130Ts based at Bahrain and Al Jubail. About 15 aircraft in total were kept busy refuelling strike and attack aircraft operating from bases in Bahrain and Saudi Arabia.

Other air arms which had varying numbers of the Hercules in the Gulf include Australia, France, Saudi Arabia and South Korea. These were primarily employed in an airlift capacity, although the Saudi fleet included KC-130H tankers and these may well have furnished support to offensive and defensive operations by fighter aircraft.

The Royal Air Force was one of the first air arms to send forces to the Gulf and these were supported by its Hercules fleet. Although the number involved was by no means as large as that of the USAF, the part played by these aircraft in Operation *Granby* (the British code-name for *Desert Shield* and *Desert Storm*) merits further examination.

RAF aircraft – principally Tornados and Jaguars – were sent to the Gulf in August 1990, hot on the heels of the invasion of Kuwait by Iraqi troops. At that time, it was essentially a reinforcement exercise, with the intention of discouraging further 'adventures' by Saddam Hussein's forces, while negotiations to secure a withdrawal went on. Irrespective of that, the Hercules was soon being used to move the supplies, equipment and personnel necessary to ensure efficient operations.

As it became clear that force of arms would be necessary to evict the Iraqi occupiers, the RAF set up a permanent Air Transport Detachment (ATD) on 30 October 1990, at Riyadh's King Khalid International Airport (KKIA), Saudi Arabia. It initially consisted of three aircraft and six crews plus engineering, movements and other necessary support elements drawn from the Hercules base at RAF Lyneham.

In the first instance, the ATD mission was to provide theatre airlift support, principally for the expanding British force, but also for other members of the Allied military coalition. It was undoubtedly a tense time for the crews that were present, but hopes were probably high that United Nations pressure would succeed in persuading Saddam Hussein to back down and remove his forces from Kuwait. Nevertheless, ATD personnel were fully aware of the possibility of conflict and took full advantage of the uneasy 'peace' to prepare and plan for a transition to war.

The in-theatre activity was broadly similar to commercial airline operations, in as much as a 'hub and spoke' concept was adopted, with long-range transports such as the Tristar and VC10 using KKIA as the main destination or 'hub'. Once there, personnel and equipment were airlifted onwards along the 'spokes' to a variety of destinations, including Seeb and Thumrait in Oman; Al Jubail, Dhahran and Tabuk in Saudi Arabia; and Muharraq, Bahrain. While they may not have been quite as regular as scheduled services, most destinations were visited daily and multi-sector missions were the rule

Once in Saudi Arabia, the Hercules flew hub and spoke operations from King Khalid International Airport to destinations such as Al Qaisumah, illustrated. PHOTO: PETER R MARCH

rather than the exception, with crews and aircraft often facing long and fatiguing duty days.

Hussein's intransigence meant that the threat of war had to be taken seriously. As time wore on this resulted in more and more ground forces being despatched to the Gulf, which placed an ever greater burden on the ATD. That, in turn, led to an expansion in size – first through the arrival of two Royal New Zealand Air Force C-130Hs and three crews on 23 December 1990 and then by the addition of more RAF aircraft in mid-January 1991. By the time expansion was complete the ATD had seven Hercules C1Ps at its disposal, as well as the pair of RNZAF aircraft.

Deployment of more aircraft coincided with the arrival of more crews. The ATD roster now numbered 14 from the RAF and four from the RNZAF, all under the leadership of Wing Commander Peter Bedford who took over from Squadron Leader Al Penney on 14 January 1991. RAF crews invariably flew as a unit and comprised six-man teams made up of pilot, 2nd pilot, navigator, flight engineer, loadmaster and ground engineer.

Peter Bedford's first action on taking command of the ATD was to take a good look at the arrangements at Riyadh, which were far from ideal. The limited amount of hard-standing was heavily congested, being shared with RAF VC10 tankers and an assortment of French Air Force tanker and transport aircraft. Other facilities were scarcely more accommodating, with operations desks and other necessary infrastructure being housed in the shell of Terminal Four alongside the French and the VC10 echelons.

The opening of hostilities by coalition air power in the pre-dawn hours of 17 January brought a temporary halt to airlift activity. The ATD remained firmly on the ground for more than a day, until the air offensive was well under way. On 18 January, though, the ATD 'reopened for business' and was kept busy clearing the backlog of requests for transport support that had accumulated during the previous 30 hours or so.

'Hub and spoke' missions continued to be flown throughout the war. Three aircraft were normally assigned on a daily basis, subject to availability and other tasking. The ATD now found its services very much in demand by the British Army, which was preparing to go on to the offensive. One of the earliest major operations undertaken in support of the Army entailed the secret airlift of approximately 7,000 soldiers of the 1st Armoured Division from an assembly area near Al Jubail to a new site in the Saudi Arabian desert. This task began on 21 January and took several days to complete,

New Zealand committed two of its five Hercules to the coalition forces. PHOTO: PETER R MARCH

with three or four aircraft being devoted to the transfer operation throughout that period.

Prior planning facilitated the process, with ATD personnel having already taken a closer look at the old oil company landing strip at Abu Hadriyah that was to be used as a loading point. This was also referred to as Landing Zone 01 (LZ01) and was quite well appointed when compared with some of the other strips used later. It featured a semi-prepared landing surface measuring some 4,000ft long by 60ft wide, with turning circles at each end.

A fairly rudimentary loading procedure was adopted, with the hold being configured in accordance with an Operation *Granby* Service Deviation. This resulted in a so-called 'flat floor' layout, in which troops boarded from the rear and sat on their kit, prior to strops being fixed across the hold and tightened over their legs and bodies. Rough and ready it may have been, and comfort was clearly not a consideration, but it had the merit of being speedy – and would have been safer in the event of emergency evacuation. Up to 90 troops could be carried in this fashion (the usual number was around 70) with a typical day's effort resulting in the movement of 700 soldiers and some cargo. Transit to the destination airfield at Al Qaisumah took 40-50 minutes and was always accomplished at low level, culminating in a 'hot' (engines running) offload. The troops were then flown on to forward sites in the desert aboard RAF Chinooks.

Special preparations had to be undertaken before these Hercules C1Ps could be used for rough-field work. The most obvious change – and probably the most unpleasant to accomplish – involved the application of rubberised underseal to the aircraft's belly. This was done to provide an extra measure of protection against damage caused by sand and stones thrown up during strip operations. Ground clearance was also slightly increased by the simple expedient of 'pumping up' the undercarriage oleos, while tyre pressures were slightly reduced to increase the 'footprint'. Nevertheless, tyres did suffer from cuts and abrasion and there were a few instances of failure. For a time, in fact, the situation was quite

Many Hercules were responsible for the transportation of soldiers to forward locations once Desert Storm *was underway.*

Top: ***Landmarks were sparse in the desert.*** Above: ***A Hercules C1P loads troops at Abu Hadriyah, January 1991.***

serious, with the ATD's stock of spares being reduced to just a single tyre at one point. Fortunately, the adoption of steel reinforced tyres saved the day and allowed operations to continue unabated.

Even though the ATD's Hercules were being worked hard, serviceability remained good throughout the conflict, helped by the policy of rotating one aircraft a week back to the UK. As noted already, only the C1P was used for 'strip' work and this derivative formed the backbone of the ATD's fleet during the crucial early phase of the war. Later, from about mid-February onwards, the C3P was also operated, but the quantity on hand never exceeded two and they were usually restricted to 'hub and spoke' services. By and large, the stretched aircraft were limited to long-haul missions, rather than in-theatre support.

Another area in which the ATD expected to play a major role was casualty evacuation (casevac) to Army hospitals in Riyadh and Al Jubail. As it turned out, British casualties were very light and few casevac sorties were flown. However, during the lead-in to battle, nobody knew what the outcome would be and a considerable amount of attention was devoted to developing and honing the procedures that would be used to transfer wounded soldiers to medical facilities with the minimum of delay. Several exercises were run and by the time the ground war got under way, everyone involved knew exactly what part they would be expected to play.

Planning for the casevac task centred around the use of Al Qaisumah airfield. Selection of this location as the primary evacuation point was because it had more than enough ramp area to accommodate several Hercules simultaneously and was capable of 24-hour operations. In addition, a back-up landing strip to the east of Al Qaisumah was available for use in the event of an emergency. This was formally known as LZ03 and was prepared by the Royal Engineers in February

Right and below: ***Landing on the hastily-prepared desert strips tested the skills of the RAF's Hercules crews to the limit.*** PHOTOS: DAVE FRY

with the aid of bulldozers, heavy roller equipment and oil. Subsequent ATD testing showed it to be the least suitable of the desert strips, with power loss occurring on take-off, probably as a result of dust ingestion. Nevertheless, it was available – and could have been used.

Preparations for casevac tasking proceeded on a 'worst-case' scenario in which the mission would need to be undertaken on a round-the-clock basis. Fortunately, the flood for which the ATD and others were prepared never materialised and only about a dozen casevac sorties were flown. Even more remarkably, they were on a 'reactive' rather than a 'proactive' basis and no aircraft ever carried a full load back from Al Qaisumah. As for the Riyadh hospital, this ended up treating little more than 200 patients and by no means all of the injuries sustained by those individuals were battle-related.

Another desert strip – alternatively known as LZ 'Ray' or LZ04 – was prepared and tested in February. Located some 50 miles north-west of Al Qaisumah, in close proximity to the 1st Armoured Division's rear echelons, this was much more heavily used by ATD aircraft, during an intense period of eight or nine days and continuing for two days after the ground war opened. As with the first lift, it was fundamentally a shuttle operation, but only two or three aircraft were assigned on this occasion. Rather than personnel, loads mainly consisted of supplies, with the Hercules being called upon to haul almost everything apart from ammunition.

Consideration was also given to other operations, including aerial resupply drops and the possibility of using hastily prepared landing strips in Iraq. As it turned out, neither option was undertaken but had the ground fighting gone on longer, both might well have been. As it was, a feasibility demonstration of airdropping was accomplished at Drop Zone 'Ray' on 22 February. During this programme, three detachment pilots (including Peter Bedford) used a variety of delivery techniques ranging from gravity extraction of one-ton containers, through harness packs to free drops from just 50ft.

Kuwait during the day was little different from Kuwait at night once the oil was ablaze.

Following the liberation of Kuwait City, it was decided to re-occupy the British embassy as quickly as possible. This duly took place on 28 February, with a pair of ATD Hercules C1Ps playing a prominent part in the Ambassador's return to his residence. Peter Bedford piloted one of those aircraft and was airborne when the cease-fire came into effect, allowing him to claim the distinction of making the first 'official' post-war landing at Kuwait City (in Hercules C1P XV293).

That mission to Kuwait was eventful. As the aircraft descended into Kuwait City, smoke from the burning oil rigs turned day into near night. It landed safely to offload cargo and the keys to the embassy itself. A few hours later, another ATD aircraft was used to carry the Ambassador back to Kuwait. This was appropriately piloted by an RAF officer of New Zealand origins, Squadron Leader 'Kiwi' O'Meeghan of No 70 Squadron.

A clearer idea of the RAF's achievements with its Hercules (assisted by the RNZAF) can be gained from study of just a few figures. In the six weeks that the war lasted, with a fleet that never exceeded nine aircraft, the Detachment flew 1,275 sorties, airlifting 7.4 million pounds of cargo and 13,912 passengers. More remarkable still is the fact that only one planned sortie was lost and that was due to weather-related causes, rather than a mechanical or technical problem with a C-130.

Nor, despite the fact that they were operating in a war zone, were there any instances of battle damage, although the

The Royal Air Force was soon flying Hercules into Kuwait City. PHOTO: PETER R MARCH

pilot of a Saudi Navy Super Puma perhaps made up for that when he hover-taxied just a bit too close to the port wing of Hercules C1P XV291 at Al Jubail on 25 January. By a stroke of good fortune, the collision did not result in any injury. However, the loadmaster probably had more reason than most to be terrified of fire, since he ended up doused in fuel that spilled from the Hercules after it experienced a sudden amputation of about 2.5ft of its outer wing.

Since the facilities at Al Jubail were modest, it was decided that a team of battle damage repair specialists would effect a temporary fix to the Hercules and this was done over the next week. On 1 February, Peter Bedford went to Al Jubail to collect XV291, flying it first to Muharraq for replenishment of the liquid oxygen reservoir and then on to Riyadh, where it remained overnight before being ferried back to the United Kingdom for a more permanent repair. Although he almost certainly treated XV291 with due care and respect during the ferry flight to Riyadh, Peter Bedford later remarked that the handling qualities of the Hercules felt 'normal', apart from it being necessary to use slight aileron trim.

Even though the war was at an end, the ATD's workload did not slacken. They were soon involved in assisting with redeployment, transporting substantial numbers of personnel from desert locations to Al Jubail, so that they could be flown back home to the United Kingdom or Germany on VC10s and Tristars. This work began not long after the cessation of hostilities and eventually resulted in the opening of two new desert strips (LZ05 and LZ06) which were positioned near the forward headquarters of No 7 Brigade and No 4 Brigade in Kuwait.

However, it was now pretty much a downhill task and the size of the ATD steadily declined with effect from 24 March when Wing Commander Bob Iredale took over the reins from Peter Bedford. On that day, two Hercules and four crews were flown back to Lyneham. Operations from Riyadh finally ended on 14 April. By then, however, a separate and smaller detachment had been organised at Muharraq and this began operations with two aircraft and three crews on 13 April.

Once again, the 'hub and spoke' concept formed the basis of activity from the new centre of operations. Two primary routes were flown regularly, one involving calls at Riyadh, Al Jubail and Kuwait City, while the other went to Dubai and Seeb. The occasional 'special' sortie was also undertaken, but demand for airlift support continued to decline as the size of the British contingent in the Gulf area was progressively reduced. Eventually, in May 1991, the ATD was finally directed to cease operations from Muharraq, thus ending an interesting and in some ways unique chapter in the RAF's use of the Hercules.

The Hercules was not left out when it came to nose art. Top left: ***'Dennis the Menace' (XV292).*** Top right: ***'The Red Baron' (XV306).*** Left: ***'Garfield' (XV297).*** Right: ***'The Fat Slags' (XV215).*** PHOTOS: PETER R MARCH AND STU BLACK

IMPRESSIONS – in war and peace

Typhoon *Gloria* was about 50 miles north of Guam island in the Pacific. Most of the WC-130E weather reconnaissance aircraft had been evacuated to Okinawa as a precautionary measure, for the storm was intense, with surface winds that exceeded 175 miles per hour. Captain Al Gideons, a veteran aerial weather reconnaissance expert with the 54th Weather Reconnaissance Squadron at Andersen AFB, Guam, was the weather officer on the last WC-130 aircraft launched to `take the pulse' of typhoon *Gloria*. Gideons, who had experienced his fair share of excitement in more than 50 penetrations of full-blown typhoons and hurricanes, as well as dozens of tropical storms, recalls his thoughts while flying into the eye of *Gloria*.

Now into *Gloria* for the first fix. It is turbulent. The radar shows many heavy returns – cumuloform clouds – with heavy rain. I must move about the flight deck to perform my duties – checking wind, observing clouds and surface wind, and taking various readings from meteorological instruments. It looks good; we're on a course for the centre. I have to hold on now because of the heavy turbulence. Things not tied down are being tossed around on the flight deck. We experience positive g forces and then negative g forces. This is a rough one. We've all been through many typhoons, but the strong ones such as this demand respect. We have to think of aircraft limitations . . . A flight bag weighing about 40 pounds suddenly flies up to my eye level. I'm holding on! Papers are scattered, work implements tossed about. Let's be careful on this one, it may be smart to get out and make a radar fix. Up to now we're okay, but if it gets much worse . . .

We want that fix; that's why we're here. We plod on. There it is on radar. We're heading straight in toward the 'eye' or calm centre. Only one problem left. The wall is a solid, circular band of heavy cumuloform clouds complete with thunderstorms, screaming winds, excessively heavy rain. Maybe hail, too? The eye is eight miles in diameter. We know we're in for a real jolt when we hit the wall cloud. It's just massive. We try to bore straight into the wall cloud. The airplane is literally tossed out and forced parallel to the wind flow around the wall cloud. Okay, regroup. Try it again, this time crabbing into the wind more. Wham!! Once again, we're rejected by the wall cloud. Again we try, this time with 40 degrees of crab. We slam into the wall. The noise from the rain is deafening. Outside, it looks like we are in a waterfall. Severe turbulence, the worst I've experienced. It happened so quickly, nothing to do but hold on and hope the airplane stays upright. It won't last long. A minute or so later and we're through it.

Total serenity, calm, smooth air . . . sunny, hot. And all around us that boiling storm. It takes constant turning to stay inside the tiny eye. What an awesome sight . . . The black, ominous wall cloud is all around but it's bright inside the eye. Looking up, there is a perfectly circular hole in the high cirrus clouds. The sunlight is pouring through that cylinder. Like looking at a bright light held at one end of a tube or pipe with you inside. Far above there is beautiful blue sky. Below, a little stratocumulus topping at about 2,000ft. The surface of the ocean is nearly calm . . . Looking under the wall cloud, the wind has churned the sea into a frenzied froth. Strange . . . how in a distance of less than half-a-mile the wind changes from calm to in excess of 150 knots! We call a storm like this a classic typhoon! It's 14 deg C warmer in the eye than just outside the wall cloud! We ask for more cool air from the flight deck air conditioner.

EC-130E 'Weather' Hercules under more peaceful skies. PHOTO: PETER R. MARCH

Back to work gathering data and readying for a radio broadcast that we'll make from the eye. We're all set up for a radio phone patch with the Armed Forces Radio on Guam. We expect many interested listeners.

Although it had already had plenty of opportunities to display its sterling qualities, the long war in Vietnam provided the Hercules with its greatest and most sustained test. While the missions it performed were seldom glamorous and while they were generally performed away from the bright glare of publicity, those who flew and loaded it know just how valuable it was. In summing up the contribution made by the Hercules, Col David R. Lewis, deputy commander for operations of the 463rd Troop Carrier Wing, had this to say in the summer of 1966.

Airlift is indispensable to our efforts. Without it, we would surely be defeated . . . The C-130 fleet lifts a good two-thirds of all the tonnage that is transported by air within the Republic of Vietnam. It operates to all types of airfields, in all types of weather, by both day and night. In my opinion, it's the only airplane. If it had been grounded, the war would have ended. The Army couldn't have gotten where they were going. Nobody could have gotten where they were going. You could have grounded the F-4 Phantom and the war would have kept going, but if you grounded the C-130, the war would have had to end. People couldn't have gotten around. We hauled people ten miles, from one airfield to another, because they just couldn't get there by land.

Comments by Col Lewis were echoed by C-130 crew members, including pilot Lt Col Tim Brady.

Vietnam was the first big test of tactical airlift and of the C-130 in particular. Many of us were based at CCK (Ching Chuan Kang Air Base, Taiwan). We'd go in-country (to Vietnam) and spend 15 days based at Cam Ranh Bay or Tuy Hoa, then head back to CCK for two or three days before going back in-country. There was a lot of griping and minor complaining at the time, but, in retrospect, it was the best flying I've ever done in my life.

In any study of American efforts in Vietnam, about the only success story you're going to find is in tactical airlift. C-130s were really the lifeline of Vietnam, particularly in places such as Khe Sanh and Kontum. They brought in the bullets and food and everything else that the forward locations needed. If they couldn't land it, they'd airdrop it. If they couldn't LAPES (Low Altitude Parachute Extraction System) it in, they'd CDS (Container Delivery System) it in from high altitude. We had C-130s go into 2,200ft fields. The shortest I ever landed on was 2,500ft. You could go into a 3,500ft strip with a good load – 130,000lb gross weight, or so.

'If you grounded the C-130, the war would have had to end.'

'If they couldn't LAPES Low Altitude Parachute Extraction System it in . . .'

Capt James Lea remembers the C-130's landing capabilities very well.

> In December 1969, aircraft commander Chuck Burnfield and co-pilot Jeff Roberts were hauling 30,000lb of lumber into Nhon Co. They mistook Gia Nghia runway for Nhon Co and landed there instead. Nhon Co was 4,200ft long and made of laterite. It was a Type Two C-130 field. The runway direction was 08/26. Gia Nghia was 2,000ft long and also made of laterite. It was not considered suitable for a C-130 landing, but they managed it. Remarks on Gia Nghia in the TAD (Tactical Aerodrome Directory) read: 'A field built on hill-top, steep drop-offs all sides. Caution: Severe downdraughts and strong wind shear possible on final approach. Runway slick when wet. 100ft overrun each end, no turnarounds'.
>
> No one on the crew realised the mistake until it was really too late. Just at touch-down, the flight engineer said, 'We aren't going to make it.' Chuck Burnfield said, 'Yes we are.' Chuck had already reversed the propellers and was already standing on the brakes. He then pushed number one and two throttles to ground idle and left three and four in full reverse setting. The aircraft then made several 360-degree turns on the runway and stopped just short of the 100-foot drop-off at the end of the runway. Several sighs of relief were emitted by all crew members, and a long period of silence ensued before Jeff Roberts looked at Chuck Burnfield and asked if he wanted the after-landing check-list.
>
> Chuck, who always did everything by the book, said, 'Give me that check-list.' Jeff handed it over to him and Chuck just threw it out the window, saying, 'There are times when you read the check-list, and there are times when you say to hell with the damn check-list.' After calling their base on the radio, the crew got off and looked the plane over for damage. The nose strut was broken. Later, another crew was flown in to fly the C-130 out. As for the lumber, it took about two weeks and 50 sorties by C-7s to haul it out of Gia Nghia to Nhon Co.

The USAF certainly did not have a monopoly on tactical support operations. One service which used the type extensively was the Marine Corps and pilot Chief Warrant Officer Henry Wildfang sums up his attitude to the KC-130F.

> I always had confidence in the C-130. The loads in Vietnam were always suspect. You hoped you were well within the weight limits and that the figures were accurate. But, sometimes, you had your doubts. With the C-130, that was never a great worry, at least it wasn't to me. I always felt comfortable with it and I thought – well, hell, if they've missed it by 10,000lb, it's not a big deal!

Capt. James Warner of the USAF also has a contribution to make on the matter of being overweight.

> John Roach was on his first night assault take-off in Vietnam and his Herky-bird was carrying two Army trucks. It was dark – a real black-out. They were rolling down the runway . . . rolling . . . rolling . . . with the end of the runway coming up fast. John pulled it up and staggered into the air at stall speed, clipping the tree tops and just barely wallowing along. At just about that time, the loadmaster piped up: 'Boss, I screwed up.' 'How's that?' enquired John. 'Those trucks aren't empty,' came the reply, 'They're each half-full of Claymore mines. We have an extra 8,000lb'. They made it, but only just.

Lt Col Bilotta was closely associated with the gunship operation and had this to say about the formidable AC-130 *Spectre*.

The Hercules excels at rough-field landings.

In my opinion, the 130 gunship was more destructive than any fighter, bomber or anything, because with the gunsights and the firepower we packed, nothing was safe. The gunships probably destroyed more enemy material than fighters and bombers because we worked at night. Some of the explosions they set up were tremendous. They'd really rock the damn aircraft.

Compared to fighters and fighter-bombers we had more firepower, we could stay up three, four, five times longer than a fighter, especially at low altitude. Plus, we had six or seven people all looking for targets of opportunity. The jet fighter would look around at 400 or 500 mph while the AC-130 could do it at 150 to 160 mph. We had the advantage. But don't get me wrong. The fighter was needed, because if we hadn't had fighters, the enemy would have shot us down.

The very nature of the gunship mission meant that the men who crewed these aircraft were exposed to hostile fire on many occasions. More often than not, evasive tactics and

The AC-130A in its 'natural' environment.

defensive equipment allowed them to make good their escape, as Col. Stanley Bramwell, an AC-130 aircraft commander with the 16th Special Operations Squadron at Ubon, recalls.

> During 1972, three AC-130s were shot down and other aircraft were hit. We flew mostly at night. I think we were one of the first to be shot at by the SA-7 Strela, which is a Russian-built, heat-seeking surface-to-air missile. It occurred north of Da Nang, just south of the demilitarised zone. We were firing at a truck and all of a sudden, the Illuminator Operator said, 'Sir, there's something coming at us.' He had never seen the likes of it before. It turned out to be a Strela. It came right at the starboard wing. We broke to the left, but it followed us. For some reason, it exploded about 20ft behind the aircraft and made quite a large white flash. The right scanner said he thought we'd been hit. I made a quick check of the instruments – everything appeared normal and the airplane flew well, but we went back to Udorn, where we found we hadn't been hit.
>
> To counter the Strela, our people devised a flare-launch decoy. The flares on the back of the ramp, which we used primarily for illumination, became a dandy decoy. We'd cut the fuse time down to about two seconds. The flare would illuminate almost immediately after leaving the airplane and the Strela would turn and follow the flare. I was shot at by Strelas eight to ten times and each time the decoy flares worked very effectively. Otherwise, I probably wouldn't be here right now.

Ellis Von Haven became the first pilot to achieve 20,000 flying hours on the Hercules. He first flew the C-130 36 years ago at Eglin Air Force Base, Florida. The C-130A was still undergoing testing and he was a pilot in the test programme. Having been based at Sewart Air Force Base, Tennessee from 1962 to 1965, he was next assigned as an exchange officer to the Royal Air Force where he trained the first RAF C-130 pilots. Von Haven began his career as a C-130 Gunship pilot in 1968 at Ubon Air Base, Thailand. He was with the first AC-130 crews deployed for duty in South-east Asia. It was in Thailand that Dave Duke, a field support operations analyst for Lockheed Western Export Company, observed Von Haven's skill as a gunship pilot.

> We used to judge pilots on how quickly they could get on target, fire and get out of enemy gun range. We were firing from a 30 degree bank and you were very exposed to enemy anti-aircraft attack during the orbit. So the object was to get on the target, roll into the bank and fire as soon as possible. Von Haven was one of the best in being able to roll into the bank, fire within the first 90 degrees of turn, hit the target and then break away. He was one of the best you could ever fly with. . .safe for himself and safe for the whole crew, said Duke.

According to Duke, the crews considered those AC-130s four engine fighters that packed a lot of power. The Herks had to be operated in extremely hostile environments without the benefit of the electronic countermeasures gear installed on many C-130s now in operation. The gunships could call for fighter types to knock out gun emplacements, that were not the primary targets.

> Although we were not supposed to do it, Von Haven was known as one of the best gun killers. He was good at spotting enemy ground fire and returning to the site and eliminating it himself. You knew his attack was successful when you observed the enemy's ammo supply exploding. Von Haven took many hits from enemy ground fire. He had some of the worst battle damage, but was always able to bring the C-130 home. On one sortie, the whole nose wheel area was shot up and badly damaged. Shrapnel penetrated the flight deck wounding the flight engineer and disabling some of the radio gear and flight controls. Von Haven managed to land the aircraft with minimal damage, said Duke.

Von Haven remained a Gunship commander until his retirement from the Air Force in 1978. By then he had accumulated 6,000 hours in various model C-130s. From the Air Force, Von Haven began his career as a commercial pilot flying L-100 Hercules for Southern Air Transport until 1989, passing the 20,000 hours milestone in December 1991 while flying L-100s for Transafrik International Airlines. Imagine piloting a Hercules continuously, 24 hours a day, for a little over two years. That's what 20,000 hours of experience would be if it were humanly possible. If a pilot flew the Hercules for eight hours a day, every day, 20,000 hours would represent nearly eight years of continuous flying. Regardless of how you look at it, this is a remarkable achievement by Lt Col Ellis Von Haven (USAF retired).

The commercial version of the Hercules, the L-100 is being operated by several cargo carriers in Third World countries. Like its C-130 military transport brother, the L-100 has demonstrated great strength in very difficult situations. According to reports received by Lockheed Field Service, on 22 January 1993, an L-100-30 taking off from Luanda, Angola, was hit by small arms fire. A rocket propelled grenade hit the number four engine. The propeller and gear box assembly separated from the airplane and the number three engine appeared to lose power. With practically no power on the right wing, the pilot was able to bring the Hercules safely around for a landing with the heavy damage it sustained.

Southern Air Transport, the largest commercial operator of the Lockheed L-100 Hercules, is no stranger to relief operations such as those in Somalia. For many years, the Miami-based cargo airline has participated in relief missions in Third World countries. Based on the company's experience and expertise in this kind of airlift, it is no surprise that it has played a major role in relief flights to Somalia. In addition to UN organisations such as UNICEF, CARE and the World Food Program, in Somalia, Southern Air operated for the Lutheran World Federation (LWF) and the International Committee of the Red Cross (ICRC). These organisations flew out of Nairobi and Mombasa, Kenya. Their initial contracts with Southern Air have provided five L-100s, three out of Nairobi and two out of Mombasa, to fly into several landing strips in Somalia.

The five L-100s average two to three flights into Somalia each day. In more than 1,000 flights on behalf of relief organisations, the Herks have airlifted approximately 35 million pounds of food, medicine, fuel and other much

Southern Air Transport is the largest commercial operator of the Lockheed L-100 Hercules. PHOTO: JULIUS ALEXANDER

Relief supplies are loaded onto one of Southern's Hercules in Somalia. PHOTO: JULIUS ALEXANDER

needed relief to landing strips near Bardera, Baidoa, Beletweyne, Mogadishu (North and International), Hergeisa, Oddur and Kismaayo. When those desperately in need cannot be reached by landing strips, Southern Air relies on its FAA certified airdrop programme as an alternative for delivering relief supplies. The airline was the first to perform airdrops into the more remote areas of Somalia. It has airdropped 380,000lb of food over Tiggieglo and Elgarad.

There is a permanent sign atop what used to be the terminal building at Mogadishu International Airport. It reads, 'Welcome to Mogadishu'. Beneath the sign are hollowed out ruins of the building, the severe scars of civil war. A few years ago this was an international airport because of tourists and other commerce. In 1989, 40,000 tourists visited Somalia pumping $8 million into the country's economy.

Since the ousting of Mohammed Siyad Barre and his 'socialist democratic republic' and the onset of civil war, this airport is one of the landing sites for cargo planes that bring food, clothing, medical supplies and other relief equipment to help save thousands who are dying of starvation and disease. The planes come from several European countries and the US and in this sense it is still an international airport.

Mogadishu, the capital of Somalia, was the location of the American Embassy where hundreds found sanctuary and were rescued by US Marine helicopters, as the Barre regime fell in January 1991. The rescue, made possible with the help of US Marine KC-130 Hercules tankers, extracted people from 30 nations and 12 heads of state. Julius Alexander reflected on that rescue as he stood on the tarmac in October 1992 after getting off a Southern Air Transport L-100-30 Hercules.

I had flown aboard the Hercules, call sign *UN Foxtrot 5* from Nairobi, Kenya. It was one of four flights that I made with Southern Air into Somalia over a six day period. This flight into Mogadishu was made on behalf of UNICEF, an entity of the United Nations. The Hercules transported 313 bundles, weighing 37,092lb. The cargo consisted of cooking pots, laboratory equipment, freezers, survey kits, essential drugs, auto mechanic tool kits, walkie talkies, first aid kits, antennas, dish ware and 40 drums of fuel. It was a full load and we had to carry enough fuel for the 1,094nm round trip. While this flight airlifted much needed equipment, most relief flights carry food as well, and some carry only food.

To secure the Hercules and its cargo, the UN and other relief organisations hire armed security who are local Somalis. The impressionable thing for me, was that the security consisted mostly of youths under 20 years of age. Not so surprising when one considers that one third of

At the landing strips, the supplies are off-loaded by hand under the watchful eye of the United Nations. PHOTOS: JULIUS ALEXANDER

Somalia's population is under age 29 and life expectancy, prior to the civil war, was only 56 years. Also hired by the UN and other relief organisations are local Somalis to unload the Hercules. This is done by hand (no fancy equipment or K loaders) from the cargo hold directly to trucks that haul the supplies to storage areas. From the storage areas the relief supplies are later distributed to relief workers for use. In the case of food, it is distributed to feeding stations.

As the last loaded truck leaves, the cargo doors of the L-100 are closing and the flight crew is starting the engines. After we are off and en route back to Nairobi, I get to talk with the flight crew during the two hour journey. The Captain for this trip is Sid Head. For him, flying these relief missions is a satisfying experience. 'It's rewarding to get the job done. Flying is actually fairly standard. The airfields are usually in pretty good shape. Half of them are concrete and fairly long ex-military; the other half are relatively short dirt strips, but the Herk is built for that and does a fine job,' said Head.

The challenge for pilots flying in third world countries, according to Head, is operating with little or no navigation aids and practically no facilities. In addition to aeronautical charts, a road map of Somalia is standard equipment for Southern Air pilots. Using DR navigation, knowing the terrain, and being on watch for the unexpected is the rule of operation here. 'So you are navigating using your airborne equipment and maps. Basically it's keeping your head up, paying attention to what you are doing and being alert,' he added.

Weather can be a crucial factor in any kind of flying but in Somalia where the airport sometimes is a dirt strip means being alert at all times. 'It can rain here a lot and the field conditions can drastically change. You may have a runway hard packed one day, kicking up a lot of dust and on the next day be in mud almost up to the axle because it rained overnight,' said Head.

Southern Air first officer, Gary Young, from Lawrenceville, Georgia, also feels that the Hercules works well in these kind of operations.

> As far as the mission goes, the Hercules is the ideal aircraft for it. We can get into small strips that you wouldn't even think of with other types. Even those that could go into these strips can't carry anywhere the load we can with the Herk, so you couldn't ask for a better aircraft. The mission is definitely necessary because the people are hurting for food and in some places the only way they are going to get it is to fly it in. Hostilities are too great to transport it across the country via trucks in a caravan, said Young.

Mike Gilkey, Southern Air flight engineer, who doubles as the aircraft's mechanic, is proud to fly these missions of mercy.

> The challenge for the flight engineer/aircraft mechanic is that you go into some pretty rough strips most of the time and the airplane can be damaged, especially around the hydraulic system that operates the brake lines. If that happens, I fix it in the field so that we can get back to the maintenance base. It's good and we like being able to take food into Somalia to help the starving people.

Wg Cdr Tony Webb AFC RAF (Retd), a former RAF Hercules pilot, describes his encounter with *Fat Albert*, as the C-130K is affectionately known.

> So, you've been chosen to fly the Hercules. When you first look at the machine, what exactly do you see? It's big; with a wing that spans 133ft; an enormous fin, the top of which sits nearly 100ft off the ground; and four paddle-shaped blades on each of the four propellers. It's also rugged, workmanlike, practical, but strangely seductive too. Perhaps you sense this because you could hardly have avoided knowing something of the C-130's considerable reputation, and because that knowledge persuades you to look beyond the familiar shape.
>
> Having moved to the Hercules from much smaller aircraft, size was the first thing that struck me; it was a longish climb from the ground up to the flight deck, via two sets of stairs. The flight deck itself was spacious and the seats looked more like armchairs than the cramped ejector seats fitted to fighters and trainers. There were two bunks at the back of the area, making me feel this was no cockpit, but something altogether different. It also had the feel of a greenhouse, with glass above and below eye level, as well as a very wide wrap-around main window. Every other surface that was visible appeared to be jammed with hundreds of instruments, switches and circuit breaker panels. There was clearly no way that any one person would be able to understand, or even remember, what they were all for.
>
> In front of each pilots' seat there stood a large control column, with spectacle-style handlebars fitted on the top. There was no clue that, one day, it would be possible to control the aircraft precisely with just a finger and thumb on the spectacles and to extract whatever information was relevant by taking a quick glance at the right instrument. However, that skill would take time to acquire and several years of experience would have to be under the belt, before such a level of handling could be attained – and the matching confidence assured.

'It's big ,with a wing that spans 133ft, an enormous fin, the top of which sits nearly 100ft off the ground, and four paddle-shaped blades on each of the four propellers.' PHOTO: PETER R MARCH

Left: *'It also had the feel of a greenhouse, with glass above and below eye level, as well as a very wide wrap-around window . . .'* PHOTO: PETER R MARCH Below: *'. . . Every other surface that was visible appeared to be jammed with instruments'* PHOTO: ANDREW MARCH

The cargo compartment seemed enormous. When empty, a long, dark cavern stretched out from 'Station 245', the wall at the rear of the flight deck. This cavern was capable of seating nearly 100 passengers, or of holding up to 45,000lb of freight, or of housing several large vehicles. It was also capable of providing the means to air-drop a very wide range of freight as well as 60-plus paratroops. On the other hand, the cargo compartment could not be called pretty; the only gesture towards appearance was coincidentally provided by the sound-proofing material; other than that, the guts of the aeroplane were hanging out for all to see: control runs, flap motors, hydraulic reservoirs; equipment stowage racks, and much more besides. When the engines were running, the area was also disturbingly noisy; conversation was out of the question, and some form of ear protection was essential. Long distance travel in a C-130 was clearly not likely to be a relaxing experience – unless one happened to be stone deaf and adept at sleeping on a vibrating bench.

The Hercules has always been the subject of fierce

'The cargo compartment seemed enormous . . .' PHOTO: ANDREW MARCH

loyalty from its crews, and perhaps especially so from its pilots. What is it about the C-130 that commands this respect? Is it just a simple reflection of the affinity that all aircrew feel for the aircraft that they fly? Or is there something unique and special about the *Herky Bird, Fat Albert* or *Charlie One-Thirty*?

Resoundingly, I would have to say yes – and not just one thing, but many. The word that springs most frequently to mind is versatility; versatility of role and application are described elsewhere in this book, but there is a particular versatility of handling, of piloting, of operating that all Hercules possess. The same aircraft, without modification, can operate effectively between the climatic extremes of the poles and the tropics, can haul up to 17 tons of cargo over a distance of 4,000 miles, can land on an unprepared 2,500ft strip at night, can provide an accurate and stable platform for high level and low level aerial delivery, and can out-manoeuvre many smaller and faster aircraft.

It also offers a dependability and reliability that is seldom found in its rivals (though few Hercules aviators would even accept that rivals exist), and an impressive degree of redundancy in its systems; in other words, a lot of things have to go wrong at the same time before a mission must be cancelled.

The Hercules also handles easily and is possessed of low level manoeuvrability that is quite astonishing for its size. On the minus side, it is not the most stable aircraft to fly by reference to flight instruments, especially in the pitching plane, and close attention is necessary to maintain accurate speed or height, while it is also a handful (or, perhaps more accurately, a footful) with two engines out on the same side. Fortunately, the aforementioned reliability means that this is a situation that is encountered almost exclusively in training and most often in the safety of a flight simulator.

It is, above all, a forgiving aeroplane and that is possibly its greatest virtue. All pilots are prone to error and some aircraft will bite back at the slightest provocation – not so the Hercules. A generous flight operating envelope can be breached without unexpected or fatal consequences. Flight control response is good throughout the speed range, and the 'feel' of the aircraft is both consistent and sensitive; a pilot gets plenty of warning when the edge of the envelope is being approached.

These are just some of the reasons why the Hercules appeals so strongly to those who are lucky enough to fly it. The combination of reliability, flexibility, ease of operation, and, above all else, its unmatched versatility, continue to convince aircrews and everyone else connected with it, that the C-130 is the exceptional workhorse of military transport as well as a major contributor to civil transport. It is the only contender for the title; the only undisputed successor to the world-famed Dakota; and the backbone of tactical mobility.

We are very grateful to Joseph E. Dabney, former Public Relations Co-ordinator of the Lockheed-Georgia Company, for his kind permission to reproduce some of the quotations in this chapter that first appeared in his book ***HERK: Hero of the Skies****, originally published by Copple House Books (USA) and Airline Publications and Sales (UK) and now available in a second edition. We would also like to thank Julius Alexander, Communications Director for Airlift at Lockheed Aeronautical Systems Company, Marietta and Wg Cdr Tony Webb AFC, RAF (Retd), for their contributions to this chapter.*

ON THE CIVIL SCENE

Facing page: ***The prototype commercial Hercules on its maiden flight.*** Above: ***Following completion of trials, the aircraft embarked on a world tour.***

Interest in a civil version of the Lockheed C-130 was not immediately forthcoming, principally due to a surfeit of other, cheap alternatives. Throughout the 1950s, the civil aviation market was flooded with surplus military aircraft left over from World War 2 and the Korean War. Airlines were not keen to purchase expensive new aircraft when they could snap up second-hand examples of the C-47/DC-3, C-54/DC-4, C-118/DC-6 and other piston-engined types at knock-down prices.

Orders from the US Air Force kept Lockheed fully committed with the military programme at first but the company did initiate design studies in 1956 for a civilian version of the Hercules. In 1959 the company was able to announce an important order for a dozen examples of the GL-207 Super Hercules for Pan American World Airways. A second order for six was placed by Slick Airways the following year but later cancelled in favour of the Canadair CL-44. The GL-207 was revealed as a larger version of the C-130B, some 23ft 4in longer and with an increased wingspan. Its four Allison T61s would each produce 6,000eshp. The GL-207 was to have a gross take-off weight of 204,170lb. Soon afterwards, an alternative version was announced, which would have been fitted with 6,556eshp Rolls-Royce Tynes. The announcement of a jet-powered Hercules, powered by four 22,000lb thrust Pratt & Whitney engines, giving a cruising speed of 564mph, was made in 1960. PanAm later cancelled its order and none of these initial civilian Hercules were built.

The arrival of the GL-207 had coincided with an increase in interest by specialist airlines for carrying freight that would not fit into converted passenger aircraft. Lockheed continued with its design work, culminating in the announcement of the Model 382/L-100. This was essentially a civilian version of the successful C-130E, retaining all of the structure of the military version but with the specific military equipment deleted. The L-100 was to be powered by four Allison 501-D22 engines each producing 4,050 eshp – this being the commercial version of the T56. External dimensions would remain the same as the C-130E, with a wingspan of 132ft 7in and length of 97ft 9in, while the cargo compartment floor of 40ft 5in gave a maximum payload of 47,990lb. As with the C-130, the rear loading ramp lowered to truck-bed height to facilitate easy transfer of cargo, through track extensions, or to the ground to permit loading of wheeled vehicles. Lockheed earmarked aircraft serial 3946 as the civilian demonstrator and obtained for it the appropriate civilian registration N1130E.

Named *One World Hercules*, N1130E's maiden flight was a protracted affair by any stretch of the imagination. With Lockheed Chief Production Pilot Joe Garrett at the controls, it took off on 20 April 1964 and returned the following day after a flight of 25 hours 1 minute, of which all bar 36

Lockheed stretched the Hercules into the L-100-20 version by adding plugs for and aft of the wing section.

minutes was accomplished on only two engines, to give an indication of the L-100's versatility. Following completion of flight trials Federal Aviation Administration certification was granted on 16 February 1965.

The Model 382B production version began to roll off the assembly line almost immediately and the first aircraft was delivered to Continental Air Services on 30 September 1965. However, the first operator was Alaska Airlines, which received the demonstrator on 8 March 1965, for service in one of the most inhospitable environments on earth. By September 1966 eleven L-100s had been ordered for a mix of civil and military operators, most of which had been delivered. Orders continued to increase slowly and by 1970 totalled 22 but by this time the original L-100 had been replaced in production by stretched variants.

As civilian freight is usually less densely packed than that shipped by the military, the L-100 Hercules was limited by the volume it could carry rather than the weight. By the simple expedient of adding fuselage plugs of 60in fore, and 40in aft, of the wing, Lockheed was able to provide its customers with the increased volume that they demanded, while only slightly reducing the payload weight to 45,805lb. The L-100-20 stretched Hercules, fitted with slightly more powerful Allison 501-D22A engines, was 106ft 2in long. This gave a 48ft 8in cargo compartment floor and the ability to carry seven 118in by 88in commercial pallets in place of the L-100's six. The extended demonstrator (N1130E) flew for the first time as an L-100-20 on 19 April 1968. FAA certification was received on 4 October 1968. The L-100-20 entered service one week later with Interior Airways (subsequently renamed Alaska International Airlines); whilst Southern Air Transport received the first new-build aircraft the following month. As the conversion from L-100 to L-100-20 was relatively straightforward, many of the L-100s were retrospectively converted to L-100-20 standard. Production of the L-100-20 continued until the end of 1980. A total of 27 was built new and a further nine L-100s modified.

A second 'stretch' of the Hercules came in 1970, when longer plugs were added – 100in fore, and 80in aft, in place of the 60in and 40in stretches of the -20. This made the Model 382G L-100-30 'Super Stretch' Hercules 112ft 8in long with a cargo floor length of 55ft 4in. Able to accommodate eight pallets or five 8ft x 8ft x 10ft containers, the L-100-30 became the 'standard' civil Hercules and remains in production today. Nearly 70 have been built so far, and a dozen aircraft extended from earlier models. The first L-100-30 was delivered to Saturn Airways in December 1970.

Several other civil versions of the Hercules have been proposed but none has come to fruition. One of the earliest was the Model 382D L-100-10, which was to have been based on the C-130H with the more powerful 501-D22A engines. Its development was overtaken by the L-100-20. Further stretches to the Hercules in the form of the L-100-50 (20ft) and L-100-60 (35ft) were proposed in the mid-1970s, but again were not produced. Other versions considered at this time included the L-100-30PX (or -31) 100-seat passenger version, the L-100-30QC cargo/passenger convertible, and the L-100-30C combined cargo/passenger variant. Similarly, the Allison 501-D22D-powered L-400 Twin Hercules was shelved.

A second stretch was introduced in 1970, making the L-100-30 112ft 8in long.

Saturn was the first customer for the L-100-30.

The discovery of vast underground oil reservoirs on the North Slope of Alaska in 1967 galvanised Hercules use in that area. The aircraft's proven capabilities of flying in inclement weather together with its huge hold capacity were particularly useful for the transportation of oil drilling and pipeline construction equipment, as well as food and fuel for those working in isolated Arctic communities. An added advantage was the fact that the L-100 retained the structural strength of the USAF's examples, giving it an immense advantage over other aircraft operating in this hostile environment.

In addition to playing its full part in the discovery and production of oil, the Hercules also has an important role in cleaning up after spillage. Oil Spill Response, an organisation set up by 20 of the world's leading oil companies, has contracted Luton-based Air Foyle to provide global rapid response transportation and emergency oil spill spraying services. Air Foyle in turn has leased a Hercules from Southern Air Transport to transport equipment and the dispersant system.

Southern Air Transport (SAT), based at Miami International Airport, is the largest civilian Hercules operator. Formed in 1946 with a single Curtiss C-46 Commando, its first Hercules was delivered in 1968 and 17 are now in service world-wide. The diverse range of tasks carried out by SAT embrace famine relief – including air drops – in Africa, aerial fire fighting and oil dispersal, transportation of livestock (including an entire zoo) and airlifting engines for other airlines. As part of the Civil Reserve Air Fleet, SAT was fully committed during Operation *Desert Storm.* It has also supported the USAF Logair and the US Navy's Quicktrans programmes. Agencies using SAT include the International Red Cross and the United Nations, while other foreign governments lacking their own tactical transport capacity are also customers. The second-largest commercial Hercules operator is Safair of South Africa, which has a fleet of ten aircraft engaged on similar duties – Safair can also claim to have preserved the Roan Antelope from extinction by airlifting an entire (tranquillised) herd to a Game Reserve.

The Hercules is proving to be increasingly popular with civilian operators around the world as a cargo aircraft, flying with airlines such as Air Algerie, Air Gabon, Bolivian Air Transport, China Air Cargo, European Air Service, Ethiopian,

Alaska Airlines found the proven capabilities of the Hercules in inclement weather situations invaluable in the icy wastes of the most northern state.

Some of the many civilian Hercules operators around the world. Above left: ***Southern Air Transport, which has the largest fleet.*** PHOTO: ANDREW MARCH Above right: ***Safair has the next biggest fleet.*** PHOTO: PETER J COOPER Below left: ***Air Algerie has a small fleet for transport purposes.*** PHOTO: PETER J COOPER Below right: ***Air Gabon had a single L-100-30.***

Libyan Arab, Merpati Nunsantara, Northwest Territorial, Pelita, TAAG-Angola, Transafrik and Uganda Air Cargo.

One of the Hercules' less well-known roles was in South-East Asia, where it was flown under the auspices of airlines such as Air America, funded by the Central Intelligence Agency (CIA). The CIA had maintained a presence in the area for many years before it first started operating C-130s on 'loan' from the USAF. In April 1961 the C-130s flew from Takhli, Thailand into Seno and Wattay, Laos but operations continued for only a short time.

Un-marked Hercules have appeared in many of the world's trouble spots.

The Hercules made its next appearance with Air America in 1965, when its high freight capacity and faster speeds made it infinitely superior to the C-46 Commando and C-123 Providers it supplemented. The Hercules were part of E-Flight, 21st Troop Carrier Squadron, 374th Troop Carrier Wing (later Tactical Airlift Wing) but had civilian crews. They flew loads from Takhli to Long Tieng, headquarters of General Vang Pao's army, where their cargo was transferred to smaller aircraft for onward delivery to tiny airstrips in Laos. Other destinations were later added, including Vientiane, Luang Prabang and Sam Thong. Initially these flights were only occasional but increased gradually until they reached a daily frequency by 1967.

Air America's loads included rice, blankets and medicine as well as articles of a more military nature – small arms, ammunition, grenades, bombs and weapons – to keep these organisations supplied. The crews were paid in cash with additional payments for hazardous duties and the entire operation was conducted under conditions of great secrecy. Hercules operations in Laos came to an end in the latter half of 1973.

While its Laotian campaign was low-key, Air America was highly visible in Vietnam, where its duties were very diverse. Starting in 1964 as a very small operation, by 1969 Air America was nominally the world's largest airline in terms of numbers of aircraft operated. In addition to fulfilling USAID contracts, Air America flew liaison and communications flights for the CIA, transported VIPs, prisoners, the Green Berets, Special Operations Groups and members of the Phoenix programme.

The 'civil' Hercules also served with another airline with CIA links – Birdair. Operating in Cambodia from the early 1960s, the airline was given a contract to supply five crews for between five and ten C-130 sorties flying into Cambodia daily, taking in food, fuel, munitions and general cargo to Pochentong, near Phnom Penh. For its operations, Birdair recruited newly retired USAF Hercules crew members, most of whom needed only minimal training to achieve operational status, including experience in the all-weather aerial drop system (AWADS). The airline's crews gradually took over from USAF personnel and made their first all-civilian crew flight on 26 September 1974. Within a fortnight the USAF's involvement had ended but Birdair operations continued for the next seven months. Five aircraft were provided by the 317th TAW at Pope AFB. They carried no external markings, with the exception of a minuscule serial number on a detachable 10in x 3in metal plate.

The build-up of operations in Cambodia was so rapid that by February 1975 Birdair was flying over 20 missions daily, these being supplemented by two other carriers using DC-8 aircraft. The Birdair fleet continued operating into Pochentong as the Communist stranglehold on Phnom Penh increased and from 3 April began to evacuate American and Cambodian personnel to Thailand on the return journeys. Deliveries of equipment into Pochentong ended eight days later although Birdair continued aerial dropping until the 17th. The spotlight then shifted to Tan Son Nhut where Birdair started removing personnel and re-usable equipment back to U-Tapao and continued these flights until 29 April

Saudia, the national airline of Saudi Arabia, operates Hercules fitted out as flying hospitals, enabling health care to be taken to the most inhospitable regions of the country.
PHOTO: PETER R MARCH

1975, when all Hercules, 'civil' and military, left Vietnam for the last time.

In association with the Royal Saudi Air Force, Saudia operates the Hercules under the designation L-100HS as a flying hospital. Fitted out by Lockheed Aircraft Services, the L-100HS contains an operating theatre, intensive care, anaesthesia and X-ray facilities. Air conditioning and power is provided by generators contained in wing-tip pods, enabling the aircraft to operate independently for up to 72 hours. The L-100HS comes complete with its own ambulance and is able to evacuate 52 patients at a time.

After a particularly serious round of forest fires in 1970 a Modular Airborne Fire Fighting System (MAFFS) was developed for the USAF. Following trials with a twin-tank version in July 1971, a five-tank system was flight tested by the Air Force Flight Test Center at Edwards AFB from September 1971 onwards: upon successful completion of the tests the USAF bought eight sets of equipment. MAFFS consists of seven airborne modules plus a ground compressor. The system sprays Monsanto Phos-Check retardant from the air, which both inhibits the combustion of trees and scrubland, and also acts as a quick-reaction

Above: *A MAFFS-equipped C-130 drops its 3,000 gallons of retardant onto a fire in California.* Below: *Hemet Valley is one of the companies specialising in fire-fighting systems; this aircraft is being operated on behalf of the Securite Civile.* PHOTO: MILITARY AIRCRAFT PHOTOGRAPHS

fertiliser to rejuvenate the damaged areas. The modules, which comprise five tanks holding a total of 3,000 US gal of retardant and two clusters of compressed air canisters, are mounted on pallets and fitted into the rear of the Hercules. The adjustable nozzles give a coverage area up to 150ft wide and 2,000ft long. MAFFS was developed by Food Machinery Corporation and is marketed by fire-fighting specialist Aero Union of Chico, California. They also manufacture several other kits for the Hercules, including a permanent conversion using computer-controlled hydraulically operated doors. Civilian operators of the fire-fighting Hercules include Hemet Valley and TBM Tankers, both of which use former USAF C-130As sold as surplus to requirements.

As part of its on-going investigation of STOL low speed handling characteristics for use in future designs, Lockheed converted L-100-20 c/n 4412 to become the High Technology Test Bed (HTTB) and commenced an independent research and development programme. In order to meet the objectives of the programme, the civil-registered HTTB (N130X) received extensive modifications. These comprised a range of test equipment, including the Lockheed airborne data system capable of up to 1024 data channels that assures quality data points are obtained during testing. The information was relayed to flight test engineers through on-board computers via an air-to-ground data link, to a super mini-computer that assisted in analysing the results. A Data Van carrying further computer equipment was transported inside the HTTB when required to support off-site testing. The first exterior modifications were the extension of the dorsal fin and installation of lateral strakes ahead of its stabilisers.

N130X's first flight in this form took place on 19 June 1984 and the all-black aircraft immediately embarked on an intensive round of testing. Over the following eight years, many more modifications were made, each to prove a further area of technology. The modifications included double-slotted fast-acting flaps to increase sink rate; drooped leading edges to the wings to allow nose-up trim for no-flare landings; composite fly-by-wire spoilers to provide direct lift control. These were used in conjunction with extended chord ailerons and rudder to enhance low-speed stability control. The strengthened undercarriage was capable of withstanding high sink-rate landings approaching 15 feet per second. Unique Allison 501D Series IV engines and new propellers producing 5,250eshp were fitted in 1989, after which N130X set several climb records.

Internally, the HTTB featured a digital flight control system to extend its STOL capabilities, reduce pilot workload in conventional flight, and improve stability. Other avionics fitted included the Lockheed Adaptive Modular Program (LAMP) with laser and charge couple device, which was later replaced with a forward-looking infra-red system (FLIR).

As part of the programme, Lockheed offered the HTTB as a flying test-bed to other aerospace companies. A number supplied systems and equipment in a co-operative venture. The test-bed was also made available to other flight research organisations such as universities.

Sadly, tragedy struck the programme on 3 February 1993 at Marietta during a high-speed taxi trial. The aircraft was evaluating responses to a port outboard engine failure when it became airborne, veered to the port and crashed, killing all seven on board, including Lockheed's engineering test pilot George Mitchell.

The Lockheed High Technology Test Bed (HTTB) during one of its early research flights.

Above: *An artists' impression of the new Advanced L-100 Freighter showing the side cargo door.* Below: *The two-crew flight deck features a 'glass cockpit'.*

The newest version of the Hercules to be announced is the Advanced L-100 Freighter. Although it retains the same external measurements as the L-100-30, the Advanced L-100 benefits from state-of-the-art technology. The clear cargo compartment width is limited by the main undercarriage bays on the L-100 which dictates that containers have to be loaded lengthways down the fuselage. In the Advanced L-100 this problem has been alleviated by the installation of a forward side cargo door measuring 138in x 108in. This allows three containers to be loaded forward of the main undercarriage in a sideways orientation as well as three aft-loaded containers, thereby increasing the container capacity of the cargo area by 20%. The L-100 is the only commercial transport capable of handling all sizes of containers used by wide-bodied main-deck freighters. The M1 and M2 containers used on the Boeing 747 freighters, for example, do not fit into Boeing 727 or 737 aircraft, thus reducing their usefulness in the feeder role. The containers can be removed from the Advanced L-100 and loaded onto aircraft or trucks within 30 minutes, thus quickly freeing the aircraft for its next task. With a usable cross-section of 126in wide x 103in high, the Advanced L-100 will also be able to continue carrying oversized loads and, with the exception of the GE90 fan section, will be able to transport all the new-generation large jet engines such as the Rolls-Royce Trent. It will be capable of handling 47,291lb of palletised cargo or 49,437lb of bulk cargo over a range of 2,000 nautical miles.

Interest in the new Advanced L-100 has been considerable and is led by the Dutch airline KLM, which foresees the aircraft being used for Europe-wide hub and spoke freight operations in place of road transportation. Other airlines to express interest in the new variant are Air France, Lufthansa and Cargolux, as well as Asian operators. Containers could be sealed by the shipper and delivered unopened to their destination, thereby speeding the process through transfer points and customs. Lockheed has identified this 'feeder freighter' area as a potential source of growth for the next few years, supported by projections of cargo growth 2% higher than that for passengers. A second field of interest for the Advanced L-100 is the small parcel services offered by companies such as Federal Express, UPS and DHL. These companies currently use aircraft such as the Boeing 727 dedicated freighter, that cost 10-15% more to operate than is projected for the Advanced L-100 and cannot interline directly with large freighter aircraft.

As well as having a greater cargo container capacity, the Advanced L-100 will also be up to 16% faster than the L-100-30, thanks to new Allison AE 2100D3 engines fitted with the new six-bladed, all-composite Dowty R391 propellers, while also improving the Hercules' excellent short-field capabilities. These enable the Advanced L-100 to meet quieter than Stage III noise limits. The flight deck has been modified for two-crew operation, and features two full avionics liquid-crystal displays, head-down and head-up displays, computers monitoring data and systems integration, colour weather radar and FADEC for power-by-wire throttles. This equipment will permit Category IIIA and manual landing operations. Further design features include improved oil-cooled generators, nacelle cooling, tail and wing anti-icing systems and a simplified fuel system with fewer valves and feeder units.

Construction of the first production Advanced L-100 – there will be no dedicated prototype – is currently planned with its first flight due to take place in the third quarter of 1995. Certification should be complete by autumn 1996, with first deliveries taking place early in 1997. Negotiations are currently under way for two aircraft. Lockheed's current market projection is for between 70 and 90 civil aircraft over the next 15 years.

Looking still further ahead more stretches for the Hercules are being studied – including a seven-container example with an aft side cargo door, and an eight-container example with side cargo doors both fore and aft.

It is planned that the Lockheed Advanced L-100 Freighter will make its first flight in 1995.

INTO THE FUTURE

The only replacement for a Hercules is another Hercules . . .

It might sound like a cliché, but there is more than a grain of truth in this statement and plenty of reason to believe that it will become a reality in the near future. While it might have been easier to use a variation of Henry Ford's famous maxim by continuing to offer customers 'any type of Hercules you like, as long as it's a C-130H', Lockheed has faced the fact that even this hugely successful variant will not go on for ever. In consequence, the company's design and engineering staff have been developing a new version on which Lockheed and its suppliers – which includes at least 21 British companies - will be able to pin their hopes with every confidence as the next millennium comes closer.

Surprisingly, however, the impetus that led to the emergence of the latest version actually originated outside Lockheed. The seed was first planted by the Commander-in-Chief of Military Airlift Command (CinCMAC) as long ago as May 1988, when he outlined his thoughts on a next-generation Hercules during discussions with representatives of the company. Until that time, Lockheed had always perceived operational capability to be the paramount criteria and the design staff at Marietta had not given much, if any, consideration to the idea of developing a less costly to operate version of its most enduring product.

CinCMAC's stated need to achieve lower personnel levels by simplifying the maintenance workload and reducing the number of flight deck crew was the catalyst that persuaded Lockheed to look closely at what might be achieved. Of course, it needed a very different 'mind-set' to examine the potential of an operating cost-driven, rather than a capability-driven, design but Lockheed personnel are nothing, if not adaptable.

It took very little time to acknowledge that the CinCMAC's idea was quite feasible. In August of the same year, Lockheed responded positively to the US Air Force, whereupon planning staff at MAC headquarters set about preparing a statement of operational need, which was sent to

Marietta in January 1989. More studies followed and further presentations were made by Lockheed, leading to another MAC request for information in June 1990.

Over the following 18 months or so, Lockheed gave further consideration to the idea and the new generation aircraft began to take on a more specific form. Key sub-contractors were approached with a view to utilising state of the art equipment already developed that could be cost effective for the new Hercules. In addition, they were invited to contribute to development of the new version as a private collaborative venture. This ultimately paved the way for Lockheed and its associates to press ahead. A decision to that effect was finally taken in December 1991, with funding of the $300-million project being arranged on a shared basis. The resulting C-130J Hercules should allow Lockheed to retain its position as the dominant force in the tactical transport aircraft market for the foreseeable future.

An operational replacements document released in 1993 reaffirmed the USAF's need to replace older C-130Es and early model Hs. In a speech at the Air Force Association Symposium at Orlando on 17 February 1994 General John M. Loh, the Commander of Air Combat Command, had this to say about the Hercules.

> The C-130s in the US are in Air Combat Command now because they are an integral to theater air combat operations, one of our major missions. C-130 crews are performing heroically every day – in south-west Asia, Bosnia, Somalia – flying in harm's way and doing a myriad of tasks, all part of regional operations. We need to upgrade the C-130 force and find a way to begin buying the more efficient and improved 'J' model. The C-130J will maximise the competence of the combat delivery mission of the great Hercules well into the next century. The C-130J is the ultimate answer for our upgrade in this mission area.

Although Lockheed, at the time of writing, has still to secure its first contract for this major new variant, the company is firmly committed to production and is already moving ahead with the construction of an initial batch of five aircraft. The first of these is expected to make its maiden flight towards the end of 1995. Assuming that the test programme is completed satisfactorily, present projections anticipate that production examples of the C-130J should be ready for delivery to customers just about a year later. In view of the progress that has been made, the C-130J Program Director, W. T. 'Bill' Mikolowsky, contends that the marriage of proven structural reliability with up-to-date high-technology components and equipment is producing the right aircraft at just the right time to meet the replacement needs of C-130E and early C-130H operators.

> It will cost much less to buy new C-130Js and operate them efficiently and effectively for the next 25 years than to rebuild and try to prolong the life of increasingly labour-intensive and costly first- generation Hercules to the year 2020. The operator will find that the performance improvements on the new C-130 and its reliability will mean that less aircraft will be required to do the same wide range of tasks as the old C-130E/H/Ks.

At the same time, Lockheed has an eye to the much smaller but indisputably worthwhile civil market. Even though civil sales

An artists' impression of the C-130J Hercules in RAF colour scheme.

have accounted for little more than five per cent of the total number built to date, the company will be offering a commercial derivative (the Advanced L100 Freighter) and is quietly confident that this will also find favour with civil customers.

Lockheed is already committed to go ahead with the construction of five aircraft. There will be no 'experimental' prototype, as all five will be completed to production standard on the existing assembly line. However, mindful of past versatility and adaptability, those five aircraft will actually emerge in four different versions, so as to allow Lockheed to offer a wide product base more or less from the outset.

A standard C-130J will lead the way. This is already under construction at Marietta and is targeted for roll-out from the assembly line in June 1995, with the maiden flight following in November 1995. It is then expected to complete much of the necessary flight test tasks and objectives, leading up to clearance for use by military operators and civil FAR certification. Test activity will also be undertaken by the second aircraft, which will be a stretched C-130J-30. The three remaining machines will comprise another stretched C-130J-30, a KC-130J-30 in-flight refuelling tanker and a civil Advanced L-100J-30 Freighter, as the commercial L382J derivative is to be known and marketed. The first parts for these five aircraft were fabricated at Marietta on 3 March 1994.

Although extensive use is made of the latest technology, the approach adopted in conceiving and designing the C-130J has been driven by the need to minimise lifecycle costs. In consequence, 'off-the-shelf' components figure prominently, with Lockheed having taken new, but well-proven, technology from such diverse projects as the F-22 fighter and V-22 Osprey and applied them to the C-130J.

Several benefits accrue from this. For the manufacturer, the use of tried and tested equipment reduces the time that will need to be spent in development. In addition, the task of actually building the aircraft will be much less complex. Although the C-130H was extensively upgraded as recently as 1990 and features a 'glass cockpit', it is still dependent upon no less than 85,000 wire termination points. The cockpit instrumentation displays must be built up in place with the correct connections of wiring being a time-consuming and very complex process. On the C-130J, however, the number of wire connections has been cut to just 10,000 and cockpit panels can be built-up outside the aircraft and tested in the avionics workshops prior to installation. Needless to say, this greatly simplifies the manufacturing task.

Cost-savings achieved in manufacture of the C-130J are exceeding Lockheed's expectations and, with the proven reliability of many of its new technology components, holds out the prospect of significant reductions in operating and maintenance costs. With defence budgets generally being reduced around the world, that is a big point in the C-130J's favour. Market research indicates that over 400 examples of the C-130J, or an equivalent aircraft, will be required globally by the year 2005. A number of potential customers, including Australia, Canada, France, Italy, Japan and New Zealand, are all showing interest, but it looks very likely that Britain's Royal Air Force will be the launch customer. The C-130J is in fact the only contender for the recently issued Ministry of Defence Invitation to Tender for an initial quantity of 30

The C-130J's glass cockpit will include head-up and head-down displays for the two-man crew.

The Dowty six-bladed propeller is being tested on an RAF Hercules (XV181) that made its first flight on 19 March 1994.

aircraft to replace existing RAF Hercules transports. The RAF is itself very keen to 'exchange' its 26-year old, hard-worked Hercules for the new variant.

So, what will this 'airlifter for the 21st Century' give the RAF and other customers for their investment? The whole philosophy behind the C-130J is based on a revolutionary change rather than an evolution. While it may retain the familiar appearance of the 2,300 or so C-130s that have gone before, it is very much more than just another Herky-bird . . .

The most visible indication of change is the powerplant and propeller. After utilising the tried and trusted Allison T56 for 40 years, Lockheed has turned to a new powerplant in the form of the same manufacturer's AE-2100D3. Originally developed for the Bell/Boeing V-22 Osprey, this variant of the Allison turboprop can generate a maximum output of 6,000shp. As fitted to the Hercules, however, it is to be flat-rated to 4,591shp. It will, nevertheless, offer benefits at both ends of the scale, generating some 31% more power, while being 18% more fuel efficient, which in turn permits the bulky auxiliary fuel tanks to be deleted.

A new propeller unit has also been selected in the distinctive shape of Dowty's six-bladed R391. Since this utilises carbon graphite composite material, it is both lighter and less expensive to manufacture as well as easier to maintain by virtue of having 50% fewer parts. The combination has already demonstrated good levels of reliability in bench running trials. Flight testing commenced in mid-March 1994 using an example of the new engine and propeller fitted to an RAF Hercules C1 that has been leased by Lockheed. Modification of the aircraft (XV181) was carried out by Marshall Aerospace at Cambridge, a long-time Lockheed sub-contractor in England and a leading member of the UK Industrial Support Group for the C-130J.

Engine and propeller trials are due to be completed by the middle of 1995. They should confirm numerous performance benefits, particularly in regard to fuel burn, which is ultimately expected to be up to a quarter less than that achieved by the T56. This equates to airlifting a 40,000lb payload some 35% further for the same amount of fuel as the present RAF aircraft. Other performance gains come in terms of cruise speed which is predicted to be around 20-30kt greater, thus giving productivity benefits; a reduction in take-off roll of about 40%, which will allow the C-130J to use airfields that are now off-limits to the type; and a 59% reduction in the time taken to climb to 20,000ft. With the huge reserve of power, the biggest difference will be noted in the C-130J's performance at 'hot and high' airfields – those that have high ambient temperatures at altitudes above 4,000ft.

Other changes are rather less apparent at first glance. New outer wing sections are to be utilised, with a view to curing the existing corrosion and fatigue-related problems. Carbon fibre composites will be used more extensively throughout the structure, in such areas as the wing trailing edges and flaps. The most striking alterations relate to the forward fuselage. This has been completely redesigned, most notably in the area of the flight-deck, which incorporates the latest 'glass cockpit' technology. Since the C-130J will be configured for two-pilot operation, the familiar navigator and flight engineer work stations have been eliminated, although a place will be provided for a third crew member, should one be required.

Four large full-colour Liquid Crystal Displays (LCDs) are the dominant feature of the flight station. They are fully compatible with night vision goggles and present information that previously required several arrays of dedicated gauges, instruments and indicators. The primary flight display is used to provide data necessary for actually flying the aircraft, while a second screen features information received from station-keeping equipment as well as advisory caution and warning system cues and messages. Engine status and system data appears on the third display, with the final LCD being devoted to navigation. In addition, each pilot has a head-up display including an artificial horizon indicator as well as information on the aircraft's altitude, speed and heading.

The overall appearance of the much revised flight station is one of almost stark simplicity, but there is plenty of room for growth, with almost 1,600 square inches of blank space available. In view of that, it is conceivable that the cockpit will become 'busier' as technological advancements occur or to meet specific customer requirements for additional 'kit'.

Two mission computers and two MIL-STD-1553B data bus interface units are provided to process the mass of data and present it to the pilots in a readily comprehensible form. A valuable new feature is the integrated diagnostics system, which identifies faults and notifies the crew of them almost instantaneously via one of the LCDs. Virtually all devices on the C-130J are digital and 'report' to the mission computer no less than 40 times a second.

Electrical power for the avionics suite is furnished by an updated system. The opportunity has been taken to install a new Westinghouse weather radar, with the C-130J using an AN/APN-241 unit (derived from the F-16's radar) that offers beacon and ground mapping capabilities. Attention has also been given to defensive countermeasures, so as to provide added protection against threats posed by radar-guided and infra-red homing missiles. As a result, the C-130J will possess AN/ALE-47 chaff and flare dispensers; the AN/AAR-47 infra-red missile warning system; infra-red jamming devices, and an AN/ALR-56M radar warning receiver. It is even possible that the unexpected weight-saving already achieved on the C-130J could be utilised to provide 'armour-plated' (Kevlar) cockpit protection.

The end result of all these changes and refinement initiatives is an aircraft that has the potential to offer dramatic improvements in reliability and maintainability, while simultaneously being much more 'user-friendly' to both air and ground crew. For the former, one particularly valuable benefit is likely to concern mission planning. This can be undertaken with the aid of computer stations away from the aircraft, captured on cassette tape and subsequently loaded in to the on-board computer system in much the same way as modern frontline combat fighters and bombers. Similar gains are expected to be experienced with regard to maintenance, especially in the field, where servicing will largely involve the replacement of faulty components – with serviceable units, before running a diagnostic check to ensure that the systems are working satisfactorily.

As well as being more 'user friendly', the C-130J holds out the prospect of significant reductions in personnel resources required to operate and service the aircraft. On the flight deck there is the potential to reduce the crew by half with the redundancy of the flight engineer and navigator. As far as servicing is concerned Lockheed estimates that C-130J operators can reasonably expect to achieve cuts in manpower resources of up to 40%.

On their own any one of these improvements would be highly desirable. In combination they should prove irresistible. They allow Lockheed to offer a Hercules that represents a quantum leap over earlier models in almost every way. In the words of Al Hansen, Lockheed's Vice-President for Airlift – "The C-130J is the most sophisticated and advanced tactical transport in the world. On-going technology improvements have made the Hercules its own best replacement..."

APPENDIX A
C-130 HERCULES VARIANTS

Prototype YC-130 taking off from Burbank for its first flight on 23 August 1954.

YC-130 – Two prototype examples of the Hercules were built by Lockheed at Burbank, California. These were powered by a quartet of 3,250-eshp Allison YT56-A-1 turboprop engines, driving Curtiss Turbo-Electric three-bladed propellers. Other notable differences from later production aircraft concerned the vertical tail which had a distinctly rounded profile at its tip; the nose undercarriage doors, which were conventional side-hinged units; and the radar, which was initially omitted, although an AN/APS-42 unit was eventually installed in the lower portion of the so-called *Roman Nose* configuration.

Despite the fact that it emerged later, the second prototype was actually the first to get airborne, making its maiden flight from Burbank on 23 August 1954. In the meantime, the first aircraft was engaged on static test duties, but this eventually joined the flight development programme and successful evaluation of both machines cleared the path for large-scale production contracts to be placed from the mid-1950s onwards.

After several years of test duty (latterly as NC-130s with the Allison company), both machines were retired from flight status and dismantled in the early 1960s.
Aircraft identities: 53-3396, 53-3397.

NC-130 – Both YC-130 prototypes were officially re-designated as NC-130s in 1959 in connection with a series of engine tests by Allison at Indianapolis. Use of the 'N' prefix indicated a permanent special test status.
Aircraft identities: 53-3396, 53-3397.

C-130A – This was the initial production version, which entered service with Tactical Air Command in December 1956 and which was later deployed with elements of the Pacific Air Forces and the United States Air Forces in Europe.

Early examples appeared almost identical with the prototypes in as much as the first 27 aircraft emerged from the factory at Marietta, Georgia with the *Roman* nose and AN/APS-42 radar, before the much more familiar *Pinocchio* nose and AN/APS-59 radar was adopted as standard. Some of the very early examples were retrospectively given Pinocchio noses, but a number remained unchanged for their entire service lives which lasted well into the 1980s. Other notable differences concerned the fin tip which embodied a much flatter profile so as to accommodate an anti-collision beacon. This was adopted from an early stage of C-130A production, while the revised sliding nose undercarriage doors first appeared on the 15th aircraft, after trials showed that the side-hinged type were prone to damage during operations from unpaved surfaces.

First production C-130A (53-3129) on the assembly line at Marietta.

Power was initially provided by Allison T56-A-1 turboprops rated at 3,750-eshp, driving three-bladed Curtiss Turbo-Electric propellers. Early experience revealed that the Curtiss propellers were less than ideal and a switch was made to Aeroproducts units with effect from about the 50th aircraft onwards, this

Early production C-130As on the flight line at Marietta – note the old style nosewheel doors.

resulting in a change of engine designation to T56-A-1A. During the course of production, improved T56-A-9 and T56-A-11 versions of the engine were introduced, with these offering greater reliability, even though the rating was unchanged. At a much later stage, from about 1978 onwards, four-bladed Hamilton Standard propellers were fitted to surviving examples of the C-130A.

Provision was also made for Aerojet 15KS-1000 JATO (jet-assisted take-off) bottles to be fitted in sets of four on each side, at the aft end of the main undercarriage fairings, and the wing sections were also 'plumbed' to take a 450-US Gallon auxiliary fuel tank outboard of the engines on each side.

Forward cargo doors were installed as standard, although these were subsequently sealed at a later date, with all cargo henceforth being loaded via the aft ramp. This was just one of a number of changes that were incorporated during the service career of the initial production model which extended into the 1990s, albeit only with second-line elements of the Air National Guard.

Production of the C-130A eventually surpassed the 200 mark, but contract changes resulted in some aircraft being delivered as RC-130As and C-130Ds. Most of those originally built as C-130As went to the US Air Force, but a dozen were produced for Australia which became the first export customer

This Tennessee ANG C-130A (54-1640) still had a Roman *nose when it visited Greenham Common in 1979.* PHOTO: PETER R. MARCH

when it accepted its initial examples in December 1958. These were finally disposed of in 1978, but two former Australian aircraft are still thought to be operational with Chad's small air arm. As far as the USAF fleet is concerned, pure transports no longer feature in the inventory, but a modest number of modified aircraft are still on strength. It is doubtful if these will survive for much longer, unlike some redundant USAF C-130As that have found a new lease of life as airborne fire-fighters.
Aircraft identities: All RC-130A aircraft except 57-0523 were later modified to pure transport configuration as C-130As. See also production table.

C-130A-II – Approximately a dozen standard C-130A aircraft were modified to the C-130A-II configuration in the late 1950s. Employed to gather signals intelligence (SigInt), few details are available of the precise nature of the equipment that was installed, but it is understood to have included direction finders, pulse and signal analysers, receivers and recorders. The entire fleet was stationed at Rhein-Main AB, West Germany with the 7406th Operations Squadron, which also routinely flew missions from Athens, Greece. One of these aircraft (56-0528) was shot down by Soviet fighters over Armenia during an eavesdropping sortie on 2 September 1958, with the remainder being replaced by the C-130B-II in 1971. At that point, they reverted to conventional C-130A standard.
Aircraft identities: 56-0484, 56-0524, 56-0525, 56-0528, 56-0530, 56-0534, 56-0535, 56-0537, 56-0538, 56-0540, 56-0541 plus one.

AC-130A – The first of the 'gunships' came into being in the mid-1960s when an early production aircraft (54-1626) was fitted with an armament array that comprised four GAU-2 7.62mm miniguns and four M-61 20mm cannon. All of these weapons were located in the cabin, firing through openings in the port fuselage side. Additional associated equipment included an image-intensifying Night Observation Device (NOD), side-looking fire control radar and an inert fuel tank system.

Testing of this aircraft, sometimes referred to as *Plain Jane*, began in June 1967 and paved the way for combat evaluation in South-East Asia during the closing stages of 1967 and early 1968. Initial combat experience proved the validity of the Hercules gunship and resulted in a further seven early production examples being converted and delivered in 1968. Although broadly similar to the prototype, they incorporated some new equipment, such as Side-Looking Infra-Red (SLIR)

The AC-130A packs a powerful punch with these M-61 cannon. PHOTO: PETER J. COOPER

First production C-130A (53-3129) was modified as a* Plain Jane *AC-130A. PHOTO: PETER R. MARCH

and Moving Target Indicator (MTI) sensors. They were soon deployed to the war zone and found useful employment in the truck-killing campaign against the Ho Chi Minh trail.

Further development of the gunship concept ensued when it was recognised that heavier calibre weaponry would be welcome, along with enhanced all-weather capability. This led directly to the so-called *Super Chicken* or *Surprise Package* prototype modification of another C-130A (55-0011). In this, two of the miniguns and two of the cannons were deleted, giving way to a pair of Bofors 40mm cannon in the aft fuselage. At the same time, new sensors were added, including side-viewing radar, low-light-level television and a laser designator/rangefinder.

After trials in the USA, the *Super Chicken* headed for the battlefield just before the end of 1969, the successful evaluation culminating in the conversion of nine more aircraft to the 'Pave Pronto' standard which differed slightly in being fitted with the *Black Crow* truck ignition sensor from the outset. Survivors of earlier conversions were subsequently brought to the same configuration and they saw extensive use in South-East Asia until the ceasefire of 1973. Inevitably, there was a price to be paid and five of the 18 AC-130A conversions were destroyed as a direct result of combat between 1969 and 1972.

Survivors were later passed to the Air Force Reserve in the mid-1970s and some remained active with the 711th Special Operations Squadron until quite recently, these including the very first production example of the Hercules (53-3129). However, the delivery of brand-new AC-130Us to the regular force seems set to result in the AC-130H being handed on as a replacement.

Aircraft identities: 53-3129, 54-1623, 54-1625, 54-1626, 54-1627, 54-1628, 54-1629, 54-1630, 55-0011, 55-0014, 55-0029, 55-0040, 55-0043, 55-0044, 55-0046, 56-0469, 56-0490, 56-0509.

DC-130A – Eight aircraft were converted to DC-130A configuration and used to carry, launch and direct remotely piloted vehicles (RPVs) such as the Ryan Firebee drone. The first two examples (57-0496 and 57-0497) were initially designated GC-130As and were modified in 1957 for trials work, which preceded operational deployment, most notably in South-East Asia where reconnaissance-configured drones were extensively used against heavily defended target complexes. Others followed in the 1960s, for combat use and for service with the US Navy in fleet live-firing exercises against unmanned targets. Modification involved the fitment of four underwing pylons to carry the drones as well as the installation of guidance equipment and operator consoles in the hold. One example is thought to still be active with the US Air Force, while three others are operated for the US Navy by a civilian contractor from Mojave, California.

Aircraft identities: 55-0021/USN 158228, 56-0491/USN 158229, 56-0514, 56-0527, 57-0461, 57-0496, 57-0497, 57-0523.

GC-130A (first use) – This designation was applied to the initial pair of Hercules that were configured to carry, launch and direct remotely piloted vehicles. Adoption of the unified nomenclature system by the US armed forces in 1962 resulted in a designation change to DC-130A (which see).

Aircraft identities: 57-0496, 57-0497.

Above: ***The USN operated this drone launcher DC-130A (55-0021/158228).*** Below: ***Originally designated GC-130As, the first two RPV carriers (57-0496 and 57-0497) were re-designated DC-130As in 1962.***

Several GC-130s, including this GC-130A (57-0471) are used by the 3700th Technical Training Wing at Sheppard AFB, Texas. PHOTO: PETER R. MARCH

GC-130A (second use) – This designation applies to a small number of permanently grounded aircraft that are or have been used for instructional duties at technical training centres in the USA. At least six examples are known to have existed.
Aircraft identities: 53-3131, 54-1621, 55-0037, 56-0517, 56-0539, 57-0471.

JC-130A – At least 16 examples of the Hercules were converted for a variety of temporary special test projects as JC-130A aircraft in the late 1950s and early 1960s. Most were from early production and they included 11 that were fitted in 1961-62 with upper fuselage radomes and range instrumentation for use from Patrick AFB, Florida in connection with development of the Polaris submarine-launched ballistic missile. On completion of test objectives, a few reverted to pure transport tasks as C-130As, but the majority were further modified to AC-130A, NC-130A and RC-130S standard.
Aircraft identities: 53-3129 to 53-3135, 54-1625, 54-1627 to 54-1630, 54-1639, 56-0490, 56-0493, 56-0497.

NC-130A – At least five examples of the Hercules have used this designation, indicating that they have been assigned to permanent special test status in connection with a variety of different projects. Despite that, three of them subsequently reverted to the standard C-130A configuration and only one (55-0022) remains active as an NC-130A.
Aircraft identities: 53-3133, 54-1622, 54-1635, 55-0022, 55-0023.

RC-130A – Development of a specialist photo-mapping version of the Hercules began with modification of C-130A 54-1632 to serve as a prototype. Trials with this aircraft in the mid-1950s culminated in a production contract amendment that called for the final 15 C-130As to be completed as RC-130As. Delivery was accomplished in 1959, with all 15 being assigned to the 1375th Mapping and Charting Squadron at Turner AFB, Georgia. Equipment included electronic geodetic survey apparatus, cameras and a darkroom for in-flight photo processing and some examples remained in service in their original form until the early 1970s. Apart from one that became a DC-130A, they were stripped of survey equipment and operated as conventional C-130A transports with second-line units of the Air National Guard and Air Force Reserve.
Aircraft identities: 54-1632. See also production table.

TC-130A – A single aircraft was completed by Lockheed as the prototype for a proposed crew training derivative with the designation TC-130A. Attempts to convince the USAF that a specialised model was needed failed and this machine was subsequently further modified to serve as the RC-130A prototype.
Aircraft identity: 54-1632.

The last 15 C-130As were completed as RC-130As, including this aircraft (57-0512).

Prototype C-130B (57-0525) during rough-field trials at Eglin AFB.

This line-up of ANG C-130Bs includes one of the 13 former C-130B-II reconnaissance aircraft (58-0711) that had the SigInt equipment removed in 1974.

The four original C-130BL 'Ski-birds' were re-designated as LC-130Fs in September 1962, including the third aircraft, 148320.
PHOTO: PETER J. COOPER

C-130B – The second major production model flew for the first time on 20 November 1958 and was again optimised for the tactical transport mission. Although it bore a strong resemblance to the initial variant, the C-130B was superior in several ways. For a start, it was more powerful, being fitted with 4,050-eshp Allison T56-A-7 engines and four-bladed Hamilton Standard propellers from the outset. In addition, the undercarriage was strengthened to make it more suitable for rough-field operations and extra fuel tanks were installed in the wing centre section. This resulted in an increase in total fuel load from 5,250 to 6,960 US gallons. In consequence, the external tanks were dispensed with.

A forward cargo door was originally fitted to the C-130B but, in common with other early versions, this was eventually sealed permanently. Other changes included provision of a crew rest area and operating weights were also increased. As with the C-130A, the major customer was Tactical Air Command (TAC), which accepted over 100 examples, but the export order book also began to take on a more healthy appearance with brand-new aircraft being delivered to Canada, Indonesia, Iran, Pakistan and South Africa.

The basic C-130B model also spawned a number of derivatives, including search-and-rescue dedicated examples for the Coast Guard and a tanker version for the Marine Corps. These are described elsewhere under the appropriate designations.
Aircraft identities: The five new-build WC-130Bs (62-3492 to 62-3496) were eventually stripped of special mission equipment and designated as C-130Bs. See also production table.

C-130B-II – Entering service in the early 1960s, the C-130B-II was employed on similar tasks to the C-130A-II, namely the acquisition of signals and electronic intelligence. A total of 13 aircraft was modified to this configuration and assigned to the 6091st Reconnaissance Squadron at Yokota, Japan, where they replaced RB-50Es used to monitor the demilitarised zone between North and South Korea, as well as other areas. In 1968, the parent unit evolved into the 556th RS and this continued to operate the C-130B-II until it was inactivated in 1971. At that time, they were transferred to Europe and assumed responsibility for tasks performed by the C-130A-II (which was withdrawn). As it transpired, they did not remain at Rhein-Main for long, being phased out by June 1974 when the 7406th Operations Squadron was inactivated and USAFE lost its dedicated SigInt resources. As for the aircraft, these were stripped of special equipment and passed to the Air National Guard and Air Force Reserve as C-130Bs.
Aircraft identities: 58-0711, 58-0723, 59-1524 to 59-1528, 59-1530 to 59-1533, 59-1535, 59-1537.

C-130BL – This designation was allocated by the US Air Force to cover the first four 'ski-birds' obtained for and on behalf of the US Navy to assist in Antarctic exploration under Operation *Deep Freeze*. In Navy service, they were initially known as the UV-1L but became LC-130Fs (which see) in September 1962.

GC-130B – Applies to a small number of permanently grounded aircraft used for instructional duties at technical training centres in the USA. At least two examples are known to exist.
Aircraft identities: 58-0727, 58-0740.

HC-130B – Entering service as the R8V-1G, the US Coast Guard Hercules search-and-rescue version was eventually re-designated as the HC-130B after brief periods of operation as the SC-130B and HC-130G. A total of 12 aircraft was obtained and they were broadly similar to the C-130B apart from being optimised for the search role. Changes embodied in these aircraft included replacement of the crew rest area by work

This JC-130B (68-10962) is operated by 6593rd TS. PHOTO: MILITARY AIRCRAFT PHOTOGRAPHS

spaces for a radio operator and an 'on-scene commander' to co-ordinate rescue and recovery operations. In addition, they were also configured to carry and drop life-rafts and survival equipment. After almost two decades of service, most of the HC-130Bs were placed in long-term storage at Davis-Monthan AFB, Arizona, pending final disposition.
Aircraft identities: See production table.

JC-130B – Use of the 'J' prefix indicates assignment to special temporary test duties and at least 14 aircraft are known to have used this designation at various times. Possibly the most interesting of the JC-130Bs were those that were used from Hickam AFB, Hawaii to recover capsules ejected by Discovery military satellites, for these featured an upper fuselage radome containing tracking equipment as well as a complex retrieval system. Trailed from the aft cargo ramp, this permitted the aircraft to snatch the capsule parachute while in flight. Other JC-130B configurations include one that was used to evaluate the Fulton STAR (Surface-To-Air Recovery) personnel retrieval system which was later fitted to the HC-130H and MC-130E
Aircraft identities: 57-0525 to 57-0529, 58-0713 to 58-0717, 58-0750, 58-0756, 61-0962, 61-0963.

KC-130B – This designation was allocated to C-130Bs of the Indonesian and Singapore Air Forces that were modified to serve as in-flight refuelling tankers. Underwing pods containing hose-and-drogue assemblies similar to those that were first installed on US Marine Corps KC-130F tankers were fitted.
Aircraft identities: Indonesia: T-1309/A-1309, T-1310/A-1310; Singapore: 720, 721, 724, 725 (ex 58-0724, 58-0756, 60-0302 and 60-0308 respectively).

NC-130B – Two aircraft are known to have used this designation, following assignment to permanent test duties. By far the most unusual is 58-0712, which was employed at the start of the 1960s to evaluate a boundary layer control system, a rudder of increased chord and single-hinged flaps. Air for flap and rudder blowing was bled from a pair of Allison YT56A-6 engines which were located under the outer wing panels and which functioned solely as gas producers. Between them, these modifications were designed to boost STOL performance, with a view to a possible order from the US Army for a derivative known as the C-130C.

This boundary later control test NC-130B (58-0712) had a short take-off and landing capability.

By the time this aircraft made its first flight in modified form, the Army was no longer interested and after a short trials programme the NC-130B was placed in storage, to await a decision on its future. Several years later, it was removed from store, fitted with conventional control surfaces and assigned to NASA for use in the Earth Survey Program. An extensive equipment suite allows it to gather data on such aspects as forestry, agriculture and land usage. It features consoles and work areas for a crew of eight operators.

The other NC-130B was less extensively modified and had previously been operated as a JC-130B on capsule recovery tasks.
Aircraft identities: 58-0712, 58-0717.

SC-130B – This designation was allocated by the USAF to cover the 12 aircraft that were obtained for service with the US Coast Guard in the search-and-rescue role. These had begun life as the R8V-1G and were also referred to for a short while as the HC-130G before finally being given the designation HC-130B (which see).

VC-130B – After seeing service as a JC-130B on satellite capsule recovery duties from Hickam AFB, the tenth production C-130B was re-assigned to the 1174th Support Squadron at Norton AFB, California in the late 1960s. It acquired the VC-130B designation at this time and remained with this shadowy unit for several years, before reverting to the standard transport configuration for further service with the Air National Guard. Throughout this interlude, it wore a basically grey and white colour scheme, relieved by a blue cheat-line and it also carried a US flag on the fin. Next to nothing is known about the nature of the mission performed, but rumours abound that it undertook courier tasks on behalf of US government agencies.
Aircraft identity: 58-0715.

WC-130B – Altogether, some 16 aircraft have used this designation to indicate assignment to weather reconnaissance duties between the early 1960s and late 1970s. Five WC-130Bs were actually built as such and delivered to the Air Weather Service in 1962, with the remaining examples resulting from modification of pure transport C-130Bs at the start of the 1970s. Electronic and meteorological sensors were housed in the cargo hold and these machines also featured an external fairing that was used to obtain atmospheric samples whilst in flight.

Eventually, following the acquisition of a number of suitably modified WC-130E/H aircraft, all 16 WC-130Bs were stripped of specialised mission equipment and assigned to transport tasks as C-130Bs with elements of the ANG and AFRes.
Aircraft identities: 58-0725, 58-0726, 58-0729, 58-0731, 58-0733, 58-0734, 58-0740, 58-0741, 58-0747, 58-0752, 58-0758. See also production table.

R8V-1G – Delivery of the rescue-dedicated Hercules to the US Coast Guard began at the end of 1959, at a time when the US forces had still to introduce a common designation system. As a result, of the initial 12 aircraft obtained by the Coast Guard, nine actually entered service as the R8V-1G (serial numbers 1339-1342, 1344-1348). For a short period, these were later referred to as HC-130Gs and then as HC-130Bs (which see).

Five WC-130Bs were constructed in 1962, including 62-3495 seen here prior to delivery.

Above: *Ski-equipped C-130D (57-0491) in its Arctic element.* Below: *With its skis removed in 1963 this C-130D (57-0486) became a C-130D-6, and when grounded as a technical training aircraft at Sheppard AFB, it became a GC-130D-6.* PHOTO: PETER R. MARCH

A desert colour scheme C-130E (64-0527) at RAF Mildenhall in 1982. PHOTO: ANDREW MARCH

C-130D – Trials of a Hercules equipped with ski landing gear were undertaken from February 1957 using a suitably modified early production aircraft (55-0021). The most obvious difference was the undercarriage, which embodied massive Teflon-coated skis on nose and main wheel assemblies, permitting use from snow and ice-covered landing strips. Satisfied with the outcome of the test project, it was decided to amend the production contract and substitute 12 ski-configured examples for conventional wheeled machines. These were given the designation C-130D and they were duly delivered in 1958, being quickly phased into support of the remote Distant Early Warning (DEW) radar sites in the Arctic.

The small fleet was later boosted by two modified aircraft, but some of the new-build machines had their skis deleted in 1962-63. Much of their service career was spent with Alaskan Air Command, before they were re-assigned to the New York ANG in 1975. Eventually, following the acquisition of some LC-130Hs, surviving examples of the original 'ski-birds' were retired in 1984-85.
Aircraft identities: 55-0021, 57-0473, 57-0474. See also production table.

C-130D-6 – Removal of the skis from six of the 12 C-130Ds during 1962-63 was accompanied by a change of designation to C-130D-6. Otherwise, these aircraft enjoyed a similar operational career, which ended with replacement by the C-130H.
Aircraft identities: 57-0484 to 57-0489.

GC-130D/GC-130D-6 – Applies to a few permanently grounded aircraft used for instructional duties at technical training centres in the USA. At least three examples exist, two having formerly been C-130D-6s while the third was a 'straight' C-130D with skis.
Aircraft identities: 57-0486 (D-6), 57-0489 (D-6), 57-0490 (D).

C-130E – Development of this version was largely driven by the need to update Military Air Transport Service (MATS) which was still predominantly equipped with near-obsolescent piston-engined types in the early 1960s. In addition, however, the C-130E was also delivered in quantity to TAC and proved very attractive to overseas customers who purchased a substantial portion of the 486 examples produced by Lockheed between 1961 and 1974.

Most of the improvements stemmed from the desire to increase payload and range characteristics. This was partly accomplished by rewriting the manuals to take into account revised load factors, which were reduced from 2.5G to 2.25G. As a result, maximum take-off weight was increased by 20,000lb to 175,000lb. Extra fuel capacity was provided by repositioning the external tanks to a point between the engines and they were also greatly increased in size, with each being able to accommodate 1,360 US gallons. Total fuel stocks therefore rose to 9,226 US gallons, although later modifications increased the figure still further, to a maximum of 9,680 US gallons with effect from the 359th C-130E.

Increased operating weights inevitably made it necessary to undertake some strengthening of the structure, most notably with regard to the wing spars, but also including skin panels and undercarriage units. The first batch of 16 aircraft entered service with forward cargo doors, but these were soon permanently sealed and were eventually removed entirely, with new outer skin panels fitted in their place. With effect from the 17th

Using JATO for a short take-off C-130E-I (64-0558) Skyhook *was fitted with the Fulton personnel recovery system..*

C-130E, the forward door was deleted. The powerplant installation was virtually unchanged from the C-130B, with the newest model using Allison T56-A-7A turboprop engines rated at 4,050-eshp.

Making its maiden flight on 15 August 1961, the C-130E began to enter service in the spring of 1962. Initial examples went to TAC for crew training tasks but the latest version was soon also deployed with MATS, whose successor Military Airlift Command eventually assumed control of all airlift-dedicated USAF aircraft in the mid-1970s. Today, following the reorganisation of US air power, the Air Combat Command exercises control over almost all US C-130Es, either directly or as the 'gaining command' in the case of ANG and AFRes units.

Apart from those examples built for US operators, just under 100 C-130Es were completed specifically for overseas use, either directly or through Foreign Military Sales channels as part of the Mutual Defense Assistance Program. Nations that obtained new-build C-130Es in this way comprised Argentina, Australia, Brazil, Canada, Iran, Saudi Arabia, Sweden and Turkey, while Israel also received this version through the delivery of former USAF machines.
Aircraft identities: See production table.

C-130E-I – Sometimes referred to as *Skyhook* C-130Es (and also as the C-130H(CT) and HC-130E), a total of 18 aircraft was modified to this configuration in the mid-1960s. The most visible evidence of change concerned the nose section, which was altered to accommodate a Fulton personnel recovery system. In the first instance, it appears the intention was to support special forces teams active in Laos and North Vietnam, but there is no evidence to indicate that the Fulton system was ever used operationally, and, indeed, it was not always installed.

Nevertheless, these machines were used for covert taskings, most commonly being employed for night and bad weather air drops of equipment, often deep inside hostile territory. This was undoubtedly a hazardous mission and was not accomplished without cost, one *Combat Talon* C-130E-I being hit by ground fire near Phuc Yen, North Vietnam and crashing in Laos in 1967, while another was shot down over South Vietnam in 1972.

As well as these duties, the C-130E-1s were employed on more conventional airlift tasks, although that was far from being their *raison d'être*. Eventually, in the latter half of the 1970s, the surviving examples were further modified for special operations duties and designated as MC-130Es (which see).
Aircraft identities: 62-1843, 63-7785, 64-0508, 64-0523, 64-0547, 64-0551, 64-0555, 64-0558, 64-0559, 64-0561 to 64-0568, 64-0572.

C-130E-II – Operational experience gained during the early days of the war in South-East Asia soon revealed the need for an effective means of directing and co-ordinating the various elements involved in prosecution of the air war against targets in North and South Vietnam. This resulted in a batch of 10 aircraft being modified to C-130E-II configuration to serve as Airborne Battlefield Command and Control Centers (ABCCC) and the first examples to be deployed to the war zone began operations in the autumn of 1965. One was destroyed in 1965 but the remaining nine were re-designated EC-130E(ABCCC) in 1977. Additional information on these aircraft and their equipment can be found under that heading.
Aircraft identities: 62-1791, 62-1809, 62-1815, 62-1818, 62-1820, 62-1825, 62-1832, 62-1836, 62-1857, 62-1863.

AC-130E – Following the success of the initial gunship version of the Hercules, it was decided to extend the programme and modify a number of C-130Es to a similar standard, so as to benefit from use of the strengthened airframe and greater operating weight. Authority to proceed with a pair of prototype conversions was given in the spring of 1970 and these proved to be the forerunners of 11 AC-130E *Pave Spectre I* gunships.

By the time the prototypes were completed in the summer of 1971, however, it was apparent that they were very different beasts and represented a considerable advance over the AC-130A, at least as far as avionics were concerned. In its original format, the AC-130E featured AN/APN-59B radar and a moving target indicator in the nose radome, a head-up display providing steering cues to the pilot, a *Black Crow* truck ignition detector sensor, laser illuminator/ranger equipment, forward-looking infra-red apparatus and a beacon tracking unit. In addition, self-defence capability was enhanced through the provision of chaff and flare dispensers and AN/ALQ-87 electronic countermeasures pods.

Armament was originally identical to *Pave Pronto*-configured AC-130As and comprised 7.62mm MXU-470 miniguns, 20mm M-61 cannons and 40mm Bofors cannons, mounted in pairs and firing to port. That soon gave way to the even more formidable *Pave Aegis* array, which consisted of two MXU-470 miniguns (often deleted), two M-61 cannons, one Bofors cannon and one 105mm howitzer.

Operational deployment soon confirmed that the AC-130E was a potent weapon for interdiction of the Ho Chi Minh trail and it also played a key role in repulsing North Vietnam's 1972 spring offensive, although one aircraft was shot down near An Loc at the end of March. Following the ceasefire, the 10 surviving examples were retrofitted with T56-A-15 engines and re-designated as the AC-130H (which see) during the course of 1973.
Aircraft identities: 69-6567 to 69-6577.

DC-130E – Seven early production C-130E airframes were modified to undertake drone launch and control operations, these acquiring extensive combat experience during the course of the conflict in South-East Asia. A maximum of four drones could be carried, but two seems to have been the typical operational complement and these were usually located outboard, allowing the inner pylons to be used for extra fuel.

Equipment was basically similar to the DC-130A model, but these machines also featured a chin radome containing a microwave guidance system in addition to the more normal thimble radome which housed tracking radar. Internally, they possessed consoles and work stations for two Launch Officers and two Remote Control Officers.

After several years of service with reconnaissance drone units of Strategic and Tactical Air Commands, the seven aircraft were stripped of specialised equipment, returned to C-130E standard and issued to the 314th Tactical Airlift Wing in the late 1970s and early 1980s.
Aircraft identities: 61-2361 to 61-2364, 61-2368, 61-2369, 61-2371.

EC-130E – Although a number of variations on the EC-130E theme have existed, only one example of the Hercules was actually built as such. This was, in fact, delivered to the US Coast Guard in August 1966 and was utilised on a global basis to

The first DC-130E (61-2361) shown here carrying four drones, differed externally from the 'A model in having a chin radome.

calibrate LORAN (LOng RAnge Navigation) equipment. The airframe was fundamentally identical to the standard C-130E, apart from featuring provision for an extra radio operator and relocated navigation stations.

After almost two decades of service, this aircraft was withdrawn and placed in storage at Davis-Monthan.
Aircraft identity: See production table.

EC-130E(ABCCC) – After more than a decade of use as C-130E-IIs, nine surviving examples of the Airborne Battlefield Command and Control Centre Hercules were re-designated as the EC-130E(ABCCC) in the first half of 1977. While this change of classification may have more accurately reflected the mission, it was not accompanied by any significant change in appearance.

Apart from an extensive array of communications antennae beneath the fuselage, the most visible external evidence of modification is provided by a pair of large ram air scoops positioned high up on each side of the forward fuselage. These provide cooling air to electronic equipment contained inside the ABCCC pod carried in the hold area. The pod is indeed a bulky piece of equipment, measuring some 40 feet in length, weighing somewhere in the region of 20,000lb, and containing work spaces for up to 16 members of the airborne battle staff. Despite its size, the pod is removable and has provision for detachable wheels to facilitate loading and unloading.

Updating of the pod has resulted in the electronic suite being progressively improved to take advantage of advances in miniaturisation and the latest examples possess secure data link and voice communications facilities while also being fully compatible with satellite communications technology. As well as improvements to the ABCCC pod, at least four aircraft were retrofitted with T56-A-15 engines, prompting erroneous reports that they were now EC-130Hs.

Despite the fact that the basic airframe is now over 30 years old, the system works well and is far from in need of urgent replacement.
Aircraft identities: 62-1791, 62-1809, 62-1818, 62-1820, 62-1825, 62-1832, 62-1836, 62-1857, 62-1863.

EC-130E(CL) – A total of five aircraft was modified to this standard for service with the Pennsylvania Air National Guard from the late 1970s onward, although one was subsequently subject to further revision to EC-130E(RR) standard. Details of equipment fitted to and mission undertaken by the *Comfy Levi* version of the Hercules are sparse to say the least but may involve jamming and acquisition of electronic intelligence. ANG personnel are responsible for flying these aircraft, which can also be referred to as *Senior Hunter* C-130Es, although there is evidence to support a belief that mission specialists are provided by the National Security Agency and that the task is performed under the direction of the USAF's Electronic Security Command.

Mission-related equipment is seldom, if ever, fitted to these aircraft at their home base at Harrisburg, Pennsylvania, but the external configuration is known to include an extensive antennae suite. Indeed, it is fair to say that these aircraft almost literally 'bristle' with aerials. Even less is known of the internal 'kit', but this may well be kept in trailers which can be quickly inserted and just as rapidly removed via the aft cargo doors at another location.

On a more mundane level, some updating has occurred to the basic airframe, with all four remaining EC-130E(CL) aircraft having been retrofitted with Allison T56-A-15 engines as well as in-flight refuelling receptacles and infra-red countermeasures jamming gear.

Although only four aircraft are still referred to as EC-130E(CL)s, it appears that at least two examples of the

Operated by the 193rd SOS, Pennsylvania ANG, this EC-130E(RR) Rivet Rider *(63-7773) is shown in its original configuration.* PHOTO: PETER R. MARCH

Landing at RAF Fairford for IAT93, EC-130E(RR) 63-9817 in its latest, very different form, with fin and underwing mounted pods.
PHOTO: PETER R. MARCH

C-130H have recently been brought to a similar configuration, possibly as replacements for two of the original machines that are earmarked for conversion to EC-130E(RR) standard. These may be referred to as EC-130H(CL)s.
Aircraft identities: 63-7783, 63-7815, 63-7816, 63-7828, 63-9816.

EC-130E(RR) – If the *Comfy Levi* version of the Hercules is not normally readily distinguishable from conventional transport models, the same claim most certainly cannot be made of the EC-130E(RR) *Rivet Rider.* Four aircraft were brought to this standard at the end of the 1970s and originally featured huge blade antennae at the forward edge of the fin and beneath each outer wing panel as well as heat exchanger devices on both aft fuselage sides and a trailing wire antenna under the tail section.

These were the most visible manifestations of change to suit this Hercules model for use as airborne radio and television relay and transmission centres, either at home in the event of a national emergency, or elsewhere, for psychological warfare. Like the EC-130E(CL), this model is operated by the 193rd Special Operations Squadron, Pennsylvania ANG.

More recently, in the light of experience gained during the Gulf War, it has been decided to revamp these aircraft (and two former EC-130E(CL)s) and install a new TV broadcast system that is suitable for operation anywhere in the world. The first aircraft to be further modified was returned to the unit in July 1992 and was significantly altered, having lost the fin leading edge blade antenna and gained four fin-mounted TV antennae pods. In addition, a pair of extremely bulky pods are positioned under the outer wing panels. At first glance, these could be confused for fuel tanks, but they actually contain UHF/VHF antenna associated with the broadcasting of TV signals.

Less obvious alterations undertaken at different times in the service of these aircraft include a change to more powerful T56-A-15 engines and fitment of in-flight refuelling receptacles.
Aircraft identities: 63-7773, 63-7783, 63-7869, 63-9817.

HC-130E – This designation was apparently used for a time to refer to those examples of the Hercules that were modified for special operations and which subsequently became MC-130Es (which see). It is possible that use of the HC-130E designation was not officially sanctioned.

JC-130E – A single example of the C-130E is known to have used this designation when assigned to temporary test tasks for a lengthy period in the mid-to-late 1960s. The aircraft concerned was in fact the very first C-130E and was used from Edwards and El Centro for trials of an unspecified nature. On completion of the test tasking, it was restored to basic C-130E standard for further service as a conventional transport with Air National Guard units in Mississippi and, more recently, California.
Aircraft identity: 61-2358.

An MC-130E Rivet Clamp *aircraft prepares to demonstrate the Fulton Recovery System.*

MC-130E – Official adoption of this designation to refer to the C-130E-I *Combat Talon* special operations aircraft came in the late 1970s, but at least three different variations on the theme are known to have existed. All are referred to as MC-130Es, but suffix letters are employed to differentiate between these subtle and not-so-subtle variations. Most numerous is the *Rivet Clamp* (MC-130E-C), with ten presently in existence. All have the so-called 'chin' type of nose radome containing AN/APQ-122 and terrain-following radar and all are able to carry the Fulton recovery equipment, although this is not always fitted. In addition, they possess in-flight refuelling receptacles, an infra-red detection system, chaff and flare dispensers and radar warning receiver gear. Four examples are to *Rivet Yank* (MC-130E-Y) standard, a fifth having been destroyed in 1981. These are basically similar, although they lack the Fulton gear and the radar installation is contained inside a standard

Pinocchio-type radome. *Rivet Yank* aircraft are also powered by T56-A-15 engines instead of the T56-A-7, which is used by *Rivet Clamp* and the third sub-variant. This was the *Rivet Swap* (MC-130E-S), one example of which is understood to have existed for trials and development work. It also lacked Fulton equipment as well as defensive ECM apparatus.
Aircraft identities (*Rivet Clamp* unless stated): 62-1843 (*Yank*), 63-7785 (*Yank*), 64-0523, 64-0551, 64-0555, 64-0559, 64-0561, 64-0562, 64-0564 (*Yank*), 64-0565 (*Yank*), 64-0566, 64-0567, 64-0568, 64-0571 (*Yank* ex *Swap*), 64-0572 (*Swap*).

NC-130E – Two examples of the C-130E sub-type are known to have been designated as NC-130Es for a series of trials associated with the C-130E-I/MC-130E project, operating at different times with test organisations at Edwards AFB, California and Wright-Patterson AFB, Ohio. Subsequently, both machines were brought to one or other of the MC-130E operational configurations and assigned to Air Force Special Operations Command.
Aircraft identities: 64-0571, 64-0572.

SC-130E – This designation was applied during the development phase of one aircraft that was delivered to the US Coast Guard for the task of calibration. By the time this machine was handed over, the designation had been changed to EC-130E (which see).

WC-130E – Half-a-dozen examples of the C-130E were configured for weather reconnaissance tasks as the WC-130E during the course of the 1960s and all were assigned to Military Airlift Command's Air Weather Service. Mission equipment was identical to that of the WC-130B model and they continued in operation in this role until the early 1990s, subsequently passing to the Air Force Reserve with which they are still active in the pure transport mission.
Aircraft identities: 61-2360, 61-2365, 61-2366, 64-0552 to 64-0554.

C-130F – Basically similar to the USAF's C-130B, the C-130F was a utility transport model acquired for service with the US Navy. At the time of delivery, they were known as GV-1Us, but switched to the C-130F designation in September 1962. Only seven aircraft were completed to this standard and these soon went overseas, being distributed between transport outfits supporting Navy activities in the Mediterranean and Western Pacific theatres of operation.
Aircraft identities: See production table.

GV-1U – A total of seven aircraft was ordered for service in the utility transport role with the US Navy from 1961 onwards. These began life as the GV-1U, but were soon re-designated as the C-130F (which see).

KC-130F – Marine Corps interest in obtaining a tanker version of the Hercules resulted in a pair of USAF C-130As being fitted with refuelling pods and evaluated by the Naval Air Test Center at Patuxent River, Maryland during 1957. This test effort proved that the idea was technically feasible and culminated in a succession of orders which eventually raised procurement of the GV-1 (as the KC-130F was initially designated) to a total of 46. Based on the C-130B airframe, delivery of the first examples took place in 1960. At the time these aircraft entered service, they were fitted with Allison T56-A-7 engines, but were later modified to take the T56-A-16 version which was rated at 4,910-eshp.

WC-130E (64-0553) operated by the 403rd AW, Air Force Reserve. PHOTO: PETER R. MARCH

US Navy KC-130F (149798) made a number of experimental landings and take-offs on the USS **Forrestal** *in October 1963.*

Although the designation implies that the USMC Hercules has a dual tanker/transport capability, in practice it isn't quite as versatile as it may appear. When configured for tanker operations, most of the hold is devoted to storage of fuel. One – or sometimes two – of the bulky tanks may be carried, with each having a capacity of 1,800 US gallons of fuel. Transfer is effected via pod-mounted hose-and-drogue devices carried under each outer wing section.

For operation as a pure cargo or troop-carrying aircraft, it is necessary to remove the fuel tanks. As a result, most Marine Corps tanker/transport units keep some aircraft in each configuration so as to be ready to meet normal peacetime taskings in each of these disparate missions. They can, however, be fairly easily reconfigured to meet abnormal requirements in either role.
Aircraft identities: See production table.

GV-1 – This was the initial designation allocated to the tanker-transport model of the Hercules delivered to the US Marine Corps. The first examples were accepted in early 1960, but not all of the 46 aircraft on order had entered service by the time that the unified nomenclature system was adopted in the autumn of 1962. GV-1s already on charge were re-designated as the KC-130F (which see), while some later machines were actually delivered as such.

LC-130F – In 1962, the four ski-equipped US Navy UV-1L Hercules aircraft used in operation *Deep Freeze* were re-designated as the LC-130F. Obtained to replace Douglas R4Ds employed in Antarctic exploration and support, they were based on the C-130B variant and used the 4,050-eshp Allison T56-A-7 turboprop in conjunction with four-bladed Hamilton Standard propellers. To permit operation from ice and snow-covered surfaces, they were given a similar ski-type undercarriage to that of the USAF's C-130D and also frequently employed RATO. One was destroyed in 1971 when it crashed in the Antarctic, but three survivors are still active alongside some newer LC-130Rs in this inhospitable region during the short polar summer.
Aircraft identities: See production table.

UV-1L – A common system of aircraft designation had still to be adopted by the US armed forces in 1960 when the Navy took delivery of four ski-equipped examples of the Hercules for Antarctic support operations. These were subsequently re-designated as the LC-130F (which see) in 1962.

C-130G – Four aircraft were obtained by the US Navy for use on conventional transport taskings in the first half of the 1960s. They were broadly similar to the C-130E but were fitted with Navy radio equipment. After only a brief period of use as transport aircraft with VR-1 at Norfolk, Virginia and VR-21 at Barbers Point, Hawaii, they were modified for strategic communications as the EC-130G (which see).
Aircraft identities: See production table.

EC-130G – Deployment of missile-armed strategic submarines as part of the US nuclear triad resulted in a requirement for an effective and survivable communications link between National Command Authorities (NCA) in the seat of government ashore and submarines on patrol at sea. This led directly to the 'TACAMO' (TAke Charge And Move Out) mission in which a number of suitably modified Hercules functioned as a link in the command and control network by receiving messages from the NCA and other sources and relaying them to submerged vessels.

The quartet of C-130Gs were the first aircraft to be given this role and henceforth became known as EC-130Gs following fitment of the very low frequency communications gear. Externally, the most visible evidence of the change in mission concerned the installation of a trailing wire antennae. This protruded from the aft ramp and was capped with a stabilising cone that bore some similarity to the drogue on tanker versions of the Hercules. In operation, the EC-130G was required to fly a special flight profile that resulted in the antenna, which was reportedly some 5,000 feet long, hanging almost vertically. At a later date, the four original TACAMO aircraft were joined by a number of purpose-built EC-130Qs, with both types eventually giving way to the Boeing E-6A Mercury.
Aircraft identities: 151888 to 151891.

HC-130G – This designation was briefly used to refer to the dozen aircraft delivered to the US Coast Guard in the early 1960s, but proved to be short-lived, with the machines involved very soon being re-designated as HC-130Bs (which see).

TC-130G – Following retirement from the TACAMO mission, plans were drawn up to convert the three surviving EC-130Gs to TC-130G standard for the trainer/utility transport role in the early 1990s. This action would require removal of specialist communications apparatus but problems evidently emerged during modification of an aircraft (151891) for the *Blue Angels*. Work on this machine was completed and it now serves with the Navy display team, but the status of the other two is less clear, although one still languishes in storage, apparently as a TC-130G.
Aircraft identities: 151888, 151889, 151891.

C-130H – Production of this pure transport version was launched in the mid-1960s and it was initially aimed at the export market, although it later found favour with the US Air Force, which continues with limited procurement for assignment to Air National Guard and Air Force Reserve units. Numerous specialised derivatives also serve with other elements of the US armed forces.

Externally, it originally differed little from the C-130E, with most of the changes and improvements being far from apparent to the casual observer. One of the most significant of these concerned the centre wing box assembly, which was re-designed and beefed-up. In addition, the braking system was also enhanced, but one of the most valuable alterations concerned the engine installation, with the more powerful 4,508-eshp Allison T56-A-15 turboprop being adopted as standard. Rocket-

Originally an EC-130G, the current Blue Angels *support Hercules (151891) is now designated TC-130G.* PHOTO: PETER R. MARCH

The 2,000th Hercules produced – C-130H (91-1231) serves with the Kentucky ANG.

The 'stretched' C-130H-30 is still in production and already serves with a number of air arms, including France.

assisted take-off provision was also incorporated when production began, only to be deleted during the course of 1975, while the opportunity has been taken to embody detail refinements and progressively update the avionics equipment during the course of the long production run.

The first customer was New Zealand, which took delivery of three examples in the spring of 1965, but sales were slow to take off and it was not until the 1970s that it really began to find acceptance. Since then, almost 650 C-130Hs have been built, making it easily the most numerous version of the Hercules. It is also the most widely operated model and presently serves with some 50 air arms around the world, a number that is confidently expected to rise, since the C-130H is still in production.

Several former Coast Guard HC-130Hs and USAF WC-130Hs are also known as C-130Hs, following removal of specialised mission equipment.

Aircraft identities – 64-14866, 65-0964, 65-0967, 65-0969, 65-0972, 65-0976, 65-0977, 65-0985, 67-7183 to 67-7185. See also the production table.

C-130H(CT) – This designation was one of several that were used for a time to refer to the C-130E-I special mission aircraft prior to their being referred to as MC-130Es with effect from the late 1970s. Further details can be found under those headings.
Aircraft identities: See C-130E-I and MC-130E entries.

C-130H-30 – Something of a hybrid, in so far as it embodies key features of the civilian L-100-30, this model is specifically aimed at military customers and began life as the C-130H(S). The most notable change concerns the fuselage, which is some 15ft longer, thus significantly increasing payload. In 1980, Indonesia became the first customer and more export sales have ensued, with others in prospect as this version is still in production.
Aircraft identities: See production table.

C-130H(AEH) – Optimised for the provision of medical facilities in isolated areas, the C-130H(AEH) is a fully-outfitted Airborne Emergency Hospital derivative, in which the hold area is given over to an operating room and an intensive care unit, while also accommodating examination and emergency treatment areas and storage facilities for medications. Electrical current for the various systems is furnished by additional auxiliary power units located in the external fuel tanks. Other distinctive features comprise high frequency probe antennae beneath each outer wing section and a retractable loop antenna

A Saudi Arabian C-130H (AEH) Airborne Emergency Hospital (HZ-MS07) at Heathrow in 1986. PHOTO: PETER J. COOPER

The most noticeable feature of this Indonesian AF C-130H-MP SAR aircraft is the observation windows that replace the port para-door.

which extends from the fuselage for communications in remote locations.

Three aircraft were completed and delivered to Saudi Arabia between 1980 and 1982 and they were later joined by five similarly configured L-100-30s and one C-130H-30.
Aircraft identities: See production table.

C-130H-MP – Maritime patrol and search-and-rescue are the primary missions undertaken by the C-130H-MP, the first three examples of which were delivered to Malaysia in 1980. A fourth aircraft was also handed over to Indonesia in 1981, but this was destroyed in an accident in 1985.

External evidence of change is limited to the provision of observation windows in lieu of the port paradrop door and searchlights mounted on the wing leading edges. In addition, palletised rescue equipment may be installed in the hold, for ejection via the rear ramp door, while surveillance apparatus includes a Hasselblad camera that functions in conjunction with the aircraft's navigation system to produce imagery featuring a matrix showing time and position of any object that is photographed.
Aircraft identities: See production table.

AC-130H – After being re-engined with 4,508-eshp T56-A-15 turboprops, the 10 surviving AC-130Es were formally re-designated as AC-130Hs in 1973. Further modification has taken place since then and they now possess in-flight refuelling receptacles, thus greatly extending the time they can stay on

Built as a C-130E and modified to AC-130E, this aircraft (69-6568) was re-designated as an AC-130H in 1973.

station. Upgrading of navigation and communications systems has also taken place, along with provision of improved fire control computers and enhanced sensors and electronic countermeasures gear.
Aircraft identities: 69-6567 to 69-6570, 69-6572 to 69-6577.

DC-130H – Following on from successful deployment and operation of earlier drone director versions of the Hercules, plans were drawn up to bring two former rescue-dedicated HC-130Hs to DC-130H configuration. In this guise, each would have been able to carry and simultaneously control a maximum of four drones.

Above: ***The sole DC-130H drone-director (65-0979) was subsequently re-designated NC-130H.*** Below: ***One of the 16*** **Compass Call** ***communications jamming EC-130Hs (73-1585).***
PHOTO: PETER R. MARCH

The ceasefire in Vietnam resulted in the project being downgraded and just one aircraft was brought to this standard in 1975-76, this subsequently joining the 6514th Test Squadron for development tasks. It was later re-designated as an NC-130H.
Aircraft identity: 65-0979.

EC-130H – Amongst the most distinctively modified members of the Hercules family are the 16 aircraft which resulted from the *Compass Call* communications jamming project. The most obvious evidence of a change in mission is the tail-mounted antenna array which incorporates a number of bracing struts, but these unusual aircraft also possess prominent blister fairings on the aft fuselage sides and extra ram air inlets in the undercarriage bays to provide cooling air for on-board electronic apparatus.

Modification of four HC-130Hs and a dozen C-130Hs was accomplished in the early 1980s and these aircraft were originally deployed with Electronic Combat Squadrons at Davis-Monthan AFB, Arizona (the 41st ECS) and Sembach, Germany (43rd ECS). Reductions of USAF elements in Germany resulted in the 43rd ECS moving to the USA to join the 41st ECS in the early 1990s.
Aircraft identities: 64-14859, 64-14862, 65-0962, 65-0989, 73-1580, 73-1581, 73-1583 to 73-1588, 73-1590, 73-1592, 73-1594, 73-1595.

EC-130H(CL) – Confirmation of the existence of this designation has still to be obtained, but at least two C-130Hs have recently been noted with antennae arrays that appear identical to those of the Senior Scout EC-130E(CL), as flown by the Pennsylvania ANG. One of the C-130Hs carried Tennessee ANG titles, while the other was from the 7th Wing, but it is not known if these units have assumed responsibility for this mission.
Aircraft identities: 74-2134, 89-1185.

Above: *The HC-130H had the Fulton STAR recovery system and extra side windows. California Air Guard's HC-130H (65-0981) was photographed in October 1981.* PHOTO: PETER R. MARCH Below: *This US Coast Guard HC-130H-7 (1708) is one of ten aircraft powered by 4,050-eshp T56-A-7B Allison turboprops.*

HC-130H – Configured specifically to undertake long-range search-and-rescue tasks, this was also the first variant of the C-130H family to enter service with the USAF, which accepted its initial example in July 1965. Search equipment on the HC-130H included an AN/ARD-17 aerial tracker device. Housed beneath a bulbous upper fuselage fairing, this was initially intended to assist with the location of manned space capsules, but was never actually used for that purpose.

Almost as obvious were the tines associated with the Fulton STAR recovery equipment on the extreme nose section. Although this accomplished several successful pick-ups during trials, it does not appear to have been employed by rescue-dedicated units. Other changes relating to the rescue task included provision of large observation windows on each side of the forward fuselage and the inclusion of a radio operator station in place of the cockpit crew rest bunks, which were moved aft to the hold area.

Rescue equipment included pre-prepared kits containing life rafts and supplies which could be deposited close to survivors in the water via the aft ramp. The ramp itself was also fitted with ten launch tubes capable of ejecting parachute flares, smoke floats and marine location markers. More recently, with greater emphasis being placed on combat SAR activities, the dwindling number of USAF HC-130Hs have acquired updated navigation equipment and cockpit lighting has also been modified to permit operation with night vision goggles. In addition, most of the surviving examples have been brought to HC-130P standard, with wing-mounted pods containing hose-and-drogue gear for the in-flight refuelling of helicopters.

A total of 43 HC-130Hs was built for the USAF, but less than 10 retain that designation today. Another 25 were delivered to the US Coast Guard. These were broadly similar but lacked the aerial tracker and Fulton STAR recovery gear, although some retained similar nose contours, while others were fitted with the more familiar *Pinocchio* nose radome. The primary Coast Guard mission is search-and-rescue, although this service has become increasingly involved in drug interdiction and its aircraft are sometimes seen with Side-Looking Airborne Radar (SLAR) and Forward-Looking Infra-Red (FLIR) pods for surveillance operations.
Aircraft identities: See production table.

HC-130H-7 – Basically similar to the HC-130H as operated by the US Coast Guard, this designation refers to a total of 10 aircraft which were delivered with 4,050-eshp T56-A-7B turboprops rather than the T56-A-15 powerplant. Like the basic HC-130H, they are fully compatible with FLIR and SLAR sensor pods.
Aircraft identities: See production table.

HC-130H(N) – This designation refers to three aircraft obtained in the early 1990s for service with the Alaska ANG in the dual helicopter in-flight refuelling and rescue and recovery missions. They are fundamentally similar to the HC-130P, but incorporate state-of-the-art navigation and communications systems.
Aircraft identities: See production table.

JC-130H – A single early production HC-130H was re-designated as a JC-130H after being reconfigured for the in-flight recovery of capsules ejected from satellites in orbit around the earth. Equipment utilised for this mission was similar to that used by the JC-130B and it was also assigned to the 6593rd Test Squadron at Hickam AFB, Hawaii. It later reverted to HC-130H standard and has since been updated to an HC-130P.
Aircraft identity: 64-14858.

JHC-130H – Two early production examples of the HC-130H operated as JHC-130Hs with the 6593rd Test Squadron on in-flight capsule recovery duties from Hickam AFB, Hawaii. Both subsequently adopted the NC-130H designation for a while, before being returned to basic HC-130H configuration.
Aircraft identities: 64-14854, 64-14857.

KC-130H – Approximately two dozen examples of the KC-130H tanker derivative have been sold to export customers over a period of about 20 years and this version is still available. Equipment is basically similar to the tanker aircraft operated by the Marine Corps and consists of pod-mounted hose refuelling units located beneath the outer wing panels, plus one or two 1,800-US gallon fuel tanks which can be installed in the hold.
Aircraft identities: See production table.

Lockheed-Georgia KC-130H demonstrator (N4237M) refuelling Bolivian AF Cessna T-37s.

One of the quartet of LC-130H 'ski-birds' that joined the New York Air National Guard in 1985.

LC-130H – A quartet of ski-equipped aircraft was purchased with FY 1983 funding and delivered to the New York Air National Guard in 1985 as replacements for the C-130D 'ski-birds'. The primary mission is support of remote early warning sites in the Arctic and these aircraft feature similar ski equipment to that used by the C-130D and the Navy's LC-130 series. Provision for rocket-assisted take-off is also incorporated in the LC-130H model.
Aircraft identities: See production table.

MC-130H – Two dozen examples of this improved special operations version of the Hercules have been purchased by the USAF, with the first fully fitted-out machine being delivered to the 8th Special Operations Squadron at Hurlburt Field, Florida in 1990. In fact, Lockheed involvement in the project appears to be limited to that of building the airframes with only the barest essentials installed, after which they are turned over to E-Systems for mission avionics and other specialised equipment to be fitted.

Instantly recognisable by virtue of the unusual shape of its nose radome, the MC-130H embodies much new equipment, when compared with the MC-130E that it will eventually replace. Foremost among this is the AN/APQ-170 radar, which features ground mapping, navigation, terrain-following and terrain avoidance modes. In addition to enhanced navigation gear, the MC-130H has a number of improvements that are intended to enhance survivability when engaged on covert operations. These include an infra-red detection system, radar warning receivers, infra-red jammers, chaff and flare dispensers and electronic countermeasures pods, while it also has an in-flight refuelling receptacle.
Aircraft identities: See production table.

The distinctive nose radome identifies this Hercules (86-1699) as an MC-130H belonging to the 352nd SOG/7th SOS. PHOTO: DANIEL MARCH

NC-130H – At least four examples of the Hercules have used this designation at different times. Two of them were involved in the satellite capsule recovery task and also served in this role as JHC-130Hs, while the other two were earmarked for modification to the drone launch/control mission. In the event, only one was configured as a DC-130H, but this and the unmodified machine later became NC-130Hs and were used by the 6514th Test Squadron from Hill AFB, Utah on various test projects. NC-130H 65-0971 was later passed to Special Operations Command and may have reverted to basic HC-130H standard before being updated to an HC-130P, but 65-0979 is

This NC-130H (64-14857) was used by the 6593rd TS for space capsule recovery missions. PHOTO: DOUG REMMINGTON

still referred to as an NC-130H. Recent tasks assigned to this aircraft include launching and directing drones during tests of early warning radar installations in the USA and Canada.
Aircraft identities: 64-14854, 64-14857, 65-0971, 65-0979.

VC-130H – Installation of a plush VIP interior led to adoption of the VC-130H designation, which is presently used by two aircraft of the Royal Saudi Air Force and two Egyptian aircraft. However, it seems that only one of the four was in fact produced

Last of 15 WC-130H weather reconnaissance Hercules (65-0985) built and one of only six remaining in service. PHOTO: PETER R. MARCH

as a VC-130H, with the others emerging from the Marietta factory as either standard C-130H transports or in a VIP configuration. Further modification to at least one of the latter machines resulted in it being brought to full VIP standard, with larger oblong cabin windows, extra sound-proofing, a comprehensive galley and far less spartan toilet facilities.
Aircraft identities: Saudi AF 111, ex 102; Egyptian AF 1281, 1289. See also production table.

WC-130H – Exactly 15 former USAF HC-130Hs were modified during the 1970s to perform the hurricane-hunting and meteorological reconnaissance missions with the Air Weather Service. Modification entailed removal of the upper fuselage radome and its associated AN/ARD-17 aerial tracker equipment, while the tines for the Fulton STAR system were also deleted although the radome itself remained unaltered, allowing the WC-130H to be easily distinguished from the broadly similar WC-130E.

One aircraft (65-0965) was destroyed in 1974, with the 14 survivors later being transferred to the Air Force Reserve. Today, only six remain in weather configuration and these are indicated by an asterisk in the accompanying list. Specialised mission equipment has been removed from the others which now perform conventional airlift tasks as C-130Hs.
Aircraft identities: 64-14861*, 64-14866, 65-0963*, 65-0964, 65-0965, 65-0966*, 65-0967, 65-0968*, 65-0969, 65-0972, 65-0976, 65-0977, 65-0980*, 65-0984*, 65-0985.

YMC-130H – Not to be confused with the later MC-130H, this model was developed specifically with the intent of participating in the abortive *Eagle Claw* operation to rescue the hostages from Iran. Conversion occurred in 1980 and involved fitment of an in-flight refuelling receptacle, booster rockets and retro-rockets to improve short-field performance, extensions to the fin and tailplane, and additional avionics in a revised nose radome. Only one example used the YMC-130H identity, but two other machines (74-1683 and 74-2065) were similarly configured, of which one (74-1683) was destroyed when the retro-rockets fired too early while still under test in early 1981. The two survivors subsequently lost the specialised equipment, with one being returned to service as a pure transport, while the YMC-130H joined the museum collection at Robins AFB, Georgia.
Aircraft identity: 74-1686.

C-130J – This is the designation allocated to a new and much improved version now being proposed by Lockheed for service with home and overseas operators. In addition to more powerful Allison AE 2100D3 engines, it will feature a so-called 'glass cockpit' with computer-generated displays in place of conventional instrumentation. Revised avionics are also to be adopted and the C-130J will be fitted out for two-man flight deck operation. At present, Lockheed is constructing a proof-of-concept prototype, but has yet to obtain a firm order, although it is optimistic that the RAF will become the launch customer by opting to purchase a version of the C-130J to replace its existing fleet of C-130Ks.
Aircraft identity: See production table.

Artist's impression of the C-130J in RAF markings.

C-130K – Based upon the C-130H, the C-130K designation actually refers to 66 aircraft purchased by the United Kingdom for service with the Royal Air Force in the mid-1960s. On completion by Lockheed, these aircraft were ferried to Marshall of Cambridge for final fitting-out with British avionics,

RAF Hercules C1 in July 1977 when the 'brown' colour scheme was standard. PHOTO: PETER R. MARCH

The first C-130K Hercules (XV176) now 'stretched' into a C3P formating with a standard C1P (XV191) in the foreground,

instruments and other equipment, before being delivered to the RAF in 1967-68.

In RAF service, they were initially known as Hercules C1s, but subsequent modification has resulted in the appearance of several different versions over the years and none survive in original configuration. Today, the main models used by the RAF are the C1K, C1P and C3P.

Hercules C1Ks are used for in-flight refuelling and feature fuel tanks in the hold and a single hose drum unit in the aft fuselage with the drogue being trailed through a cut-out in the rear ramp. Six aircraft were brought to this standard in 1982 for service in the Falkland Islands and five still operate as such.

Hercules C1Ps are essentially C1s with in-flight refuelling probes situated above the upper fuselage section, so as to extend range and payload capability. Approximately 25 aircraft were modified in this fashion and most of these remain in service at the time of writing, although some have been further updated

Above: *There is no other C-130 as distinctive as the Hercules W2 (XV208)* **Snoopy.** PHOTO: PETER R. MARCH Below: **Orange Blossom** *ESM equipped Hercules C1K refuelling a Phantom FGR2 of No 74 Squadron in November 1991.* PHOTO: BOB ARCHER

to incorporate *Orange Blossom* electronic support measures (ESM) equipment contained in slender pods beneath the wing tips.

The desire to increase payload capability was directly responsible for the appearance of the stretched C3 model, which is some 15-foot longer than the C1. A prototype conversion was done by Lockheed at Marietta in 1979 and successful testing of this aircraft (XV223) cleared the way for 29 more to be modified by Marshall at Cambridge in the first half of the 1980s. Subsequently, all 30 were given in-flight refuelling probes and re-designated as C3Ps and most of these are still active, although consideration is now being given towards finding a replacement for the entire fleet which is ageing rapidly.

One other version is also flown by the RAF, this being the highly distinctive W2, which undertakes weather reconnaissance with the Meteorological Research Flight. Flown for the first time in March 1973, it features an 18-foot long instrumentation probe in place of the normal nose radar, which has been repositioned in a bulbous fairing above the cockpit. Other mission-related equipment includes underwing pods used to obtain weather and other data, as well as operator consoles in the hold area which are monitored by personnel from the Meteorological Office.

Aircraft identities: See production table.

A standard **Pinocchio** *nose distinguishes the HC-130N from the earlier HC-130P.* PHOTO: PETER R. MARCH

HC-130N – Although its designation precedes that of the HC-130P, the HC-130N actually came on to the scene somewhat later, with the 15 aircraft that were produced all being delivered to rescue-dedicated units of the Military Airlift Command during the course of 1970. Like the HC-130P, they were based on the C-130H airframe and were configured from the outset with the capability to refuel Air Rescue Service helicopters in flight. This was achieved through the fitment of outboard pods containing hose-and-drogue equipment.

Although they were fitted with the AN/ARD-17 aerial tracking system, the HC-130Ns lacked the Fulton personnel recovery gear and differed from other rescue-dedicated versions of the Hercules in having standard *Pinocchio*-type nose radomes. All 15 aircraft remain active, primarily in the combat SAR role with regular force Special Operations Squadrons and AFRes rescue squadrons.

Aircraft identities: See production table.

HC-130P – The development and deployment of helicopters with the ability to be refuelled in flight was the major factor behind the emergence of the HC-130P model which entered

Twenty new-built HC-130Ps were delivered in 1966-67 including this aircraft (66-0220). PHOTO: PETER R. MARCH

service in late 1966 and was very quickly deployed to the war zone in South-East Asia. Featuring the upper fuselage AN/ARD-17 aerial tracker and the Fulton STAR personnel retrieval system of the HC-130H, it was also fitted with pod-mounted hose-and-drogue refuelling gear under each outer wing section.

Some 20 new-build examples of the HC-130P were originally obtained by the USAF in 1966-67, while about a dozen HC-130Hs were later updated to this configuration, gaining refuelling pods and 'plumbing' to let them refuel helicopters in flight.
Aircraft identities: 64-14853, 64-14854, 64-14856, 64-14858, 64-14860, 64-14863 to 64-14865, 65-0971, 65-0973, 65-0975, 65-0978, 65-0987. See also production table.

EC-130Q – Having modified a handful of EC-130G aircraft for the task of communicating with its ballistic missile submarine force, the US Navy next obtained a purpose-built version of the Hercules to perform this mission. This was the EC-130Q and 18 examples of this sub-type were eventually delivered between 1968 and 1984. It was based on the C-130H airframe, but featured the more powerful T56-A-16 engines and embodied a more complex communications suite that included twin trailing antennae situated in the extreme tail section and aft cargo ramp.

Electronic surveillance measures pods were also located on the wing-tips and progressive updating of the communications apparatus was accomplished in conjunction with measures to 'harden' the aircraft against electro-magnetic pulse effects such as occur in the wake of a nuclear detonation. With effect from shortly before the end of the 1980s, these aircraft were replaced by the Boeing E-6A. Most were retired, but some have been given a fresh lease of life as TC-130Q utility transports and trainers.
Aircraft identities: See production table.

TC-130Q – Following retirement from the communications role and removal of specialised electronic equipment, a few EC-130Qs were reassigned to support missions and re-designated as TC-130Qs.
Aircraft identities: 156170, 156174, 159348.

KC-130R – Attrition and the need for additional tanker/transport resources resulted in the Marine Corps deciding to order 14 more tanker-configured KC-130Rs in the early 1970s and these were duly delivered between September 1975 and mid-1978. Based on the airframe of the C-130H model, they were fitted with 4,910-eshp T56-A-16 engines and utilised the pod-mounted hose-and-drogue system to accomplish fuel transfer. However, they were somewhat more

One of 14 KC-130Rs operated by the USMC refuelling a development YAV-8B Harrier.

The last of the 18 EC-130Qs (162313) used by the US Navy to communicate with its nuclear submarines. It featured wing-tip ESM pods. PHOTO: JOHN DUNNELL

Used for Antarctic support duties by VXE-6, this LC-130R (159131) is one of five in service with the US Navy. PHOTO: LINDSAY PEACOCK

productive than the earlier KC-130F, for the new version had significantly greater fuel capacity, which had risen from 10,560 US gallons to no less than 13,280 US gallons.
Aircraft identities: See production table.

LC-130R – Based on the C-130H airframe, but powered by 4,910-eshp T56-A-16 turboprops, the LC-130R was the second ski-equipped sub-type to be operated by the US Navy on Antarctic exploration support duties. The first example was delivered in November 1968 but was destroyed in a crash at the South Pole in 1973, not long before the first of five additional machines was obtained with National Science Foundation funds. Despite that, all five are actually flown by the US Navy's VXE-6 squadron.
Aircraft identities: See production table.

RC-130S – One of the more bizarre adaptations of the Hercules as well as one of the least successful, the RC-130S *Bias Hunter* (Battlefield Illumination Airborne System) evolved as part of the USAF's *Shed Light* programme in 1967. This was intended to result in enhanced night operating capability, particularly with a view to interdiction of the celebrated Ho Chi Minh trail.

For the Hercules, it basically involved the installation of bulky fairings on each side of the forward fuselage of the aircraft. These each contained a battery of no fewer than 56 searchlights, while the aircraft was also fitted with other sensors to assist in the detection of enemy forces on the ground. Modification of four aircraft was initially planned but only two actually received the package, both being former JC-130As.

Trials with the system in 1968 confirmed that *Bias Hunter* worked well – in the purely theoretical sense of the term. On a

This C-130T (164762) is operated by US Navy VR-54 Squadron and based at New Orleans. PHOTO: PETER J. COOPER

Still in production for the US Marine Corps, this KC-130T has improved avionics and more powerful Allison T56-A-423 engines,
PHOTO: PETER R. MARCH

more practical and pragmatic note, it soon became evident that the concept was badly flawed, in so far as it was necessary to orbit at low altitude to achieve satisfactory levels of illumination. Having determined that, it did not require too much of a leap of the imagination to realise that these flying searchlights would very quickly come under heavy and concentrated fire from hostile gunners, or that their chances of prolonged survival in the face of such fire would be minimal. In consequence, the *Bias Hunter* project was dropped, with both RC-130S aircraft reverting to the pure transport role as C-130As.
Aircraft identities: 56-0493, 56-0497.

C-130T – At least 12 examples of the C-130T have been ordered for service with US Navy Reserve logistics support squadrons and it is possible that as many as 20 will eventually be obtained during the course of the 1990s. Fundamentally similar to the C-130H, the engine installation has been changed and these aircraft are fitted with the 4,910-eshp T56-A-423 turboprop as well as updated avionics. The first example was handed over to VR-54 at New Orleans, Louisiana in August 1991.
Aircraft identities: See production table.

KC-130T – Continued procurement of tanker/transport versions of the Hercules for the Marine Corps resulted in the advent of the KC-130T in the mid-1980s. This is based on the C-130H airframe but differs in being powered by Allison T56-A-423 engines rated at 4,910-eshp, other improvements centering around updating of the avionics suite to incorporate a new autopilot, AN/APS-133 search radar, an inertial navigation system plus Omega and TACAN. Procurement of the KC-130T continues at a slow rate, with two aircraft of this type having been acquired annually for the past several years and more are expected to join the 20 or so examples that are presently flown by two Reserve squadrons.
Aircraft identities: See production table.

KC-130T-30 – Two examples of this derivative were handed over to the US Marine Corps Reserve tanker/transport unit at Glenview, Illinois in late 1991, these differing from previous models in that they have stretched fuselages and are some 15-foot longer than the standard tanker. This in turn increases fuel capacity and raises the amount that may be passed to receiver aircraft via the wing-mounted refuelling pods. At the time of writing, no further orders have been placed but it is possible that more KC-130T-30s will be acquired at some future date.
Aircraft identities: See production table.

AC-130U – Moves to acquire a new gunship version of the Hercules began in the latter half of the 1980s and paved the way

This AC-130U was developed in the latter half of the 1980s with the latest 'state of the art' electronics and fire-control systems.

for the placing of contracts covering the supply of 12 AC-130Us to the USAF's special operations force during the first half of the present decade. Responsibility for integrating the avionics systems has been assigned to Rockwell and the first basic C-130H airframe was flown from Marietta to Palmdale in July 1988 for fitting out. It eventually emerged as an AC-130U more than two years later, in December 1990 and was then assigned to the Air Force Flight Test Center at Edwards AFB for test purposes.

Armament has actually been reduced on the AC-130U, but fire-power capability remains impressive, with single examples of the GAU-12/U 25mm cannon, 40mm Bofors gun and 105mm howitzer being fitted as the standard weapons. Attention has also been paid to updating the sensor suite, which includes AN/APG-80 digital fire control radar, AN/AAQ-117 forward-looking infra-red and an All-Active Low Light Level TV set, but the familiar *Black Crow* truck ignition sensor of earlier gunships has been omitted. Inputs from the various sensors are processed by IBM IP-102 computers at the Battle Management Center in the hold, but provision has been made for the 'Mark One eyeball', with observer stations on the rear ramp and starboard forward fuselage side.

Spectra ceramic armour is also used to enhance survivability in the event of taking battle damage, while defensive equipment includes chaff and flare dispensers, infra-red countermeasures and jammers. Delivery of these aircraft is expected to result in the AC-130Hs being passed on to the Air Force Reserve and the surviving AC-130As will then be retired from service.
Aircraft identities: See production table.

EC-130V – Having operated several US Navy Grumman E-2C Hawkeye early-warning aircraft on surveillance operations intended to cut the flow of drugs into the southern USA, the US Coast Guard soon reached the conclusion that it required a platform with similar detection capabilities but possessing greater endurance. This led directly to development of the EC-130V, with a single example of the HC-130H being chosen for modification as a test bed.

Conversion work was undertaken by General Dynamics at Fort Worth, Texas and this aircraft flew for the first time in modified form in July 1991, thereafter passing to the Naval Air Test Center at Patuxent River for service assessment. The most obvious alteration arose from installation of the AN/APS-145 surveillance radar, which is almost identical to the array fitted to the E-2C. As with the Hawkeye, this is contained in a large rotating dome above the aft fuselage section, with this and its supporting struts and fairings being bound to affect aircraft performance.

Other modifications are less apparent and include additional intakes for cooling of on-board electronic equipment, as well as unidentified antennae fairings on both sides of the forward fuselage and above the nose radome ahead of the cockpit. Pallet-mounted displays and consoles sited in the hold area enable the EC-130V to carry up to three system operators.
Aircraft identity: 1721

L-100 – Earmarked specifically for use by commercial operators, the L-100 series has been reasonably successful, with more than 100 having been produced since this derivative first flew in prototype form in April 1964. The prototype was similar to the C-130E, but lacked the underwing auxiliary fuel tanks and other specialised military equipment. Federal Aviation Administration certification followed in February 1965 and Lockheed completed 21 production examples of the original

Flown for the first time in July 1991, the US Coast Guard's EC-130V (1721) has been developed for anti-drug smuggling surveillance operations. PHOTO: JAMIE HUNTER

The first airline to fly the L-100 was Atlanta-based Delta Airlines that leased this aircraft from Lockheed.

L100 series by the end of 1968. Today, only one still flies in its original format with the Pakistan Air Force. Of the remainder, 13 (including the prototype) were brought to later 'stretched' standards and eight were destroyed in accidents.

The 'stretch' programme actually resulted in the appearance of two other versions. The first was the L-100-20, which was some 8.3-feet (100in) longer than the original civil Hercules. This made its début in the autumn of 1968 and 27 aircraft had been completed for civil and military customers when production terminated in 1980. Since then, Lockheed has continued to build the L-100-30, which featured another 6.7ft (80in) extension to fuselage length. Sales have been steady, but not startling, since this first appeared in 1970 and close to 70 have now been completed, with production apparently set to continue for the time being.
Aircraft identities: See production table.

Advanced L-100 Freighter – A commercial version of the C-130J, currently named the Advanced L-100 Freighter, is planned for introduction concurrent with the J model.

C-130 VARIANT – TOTALS

Variant	Total	Variant	Total	Variant	Total
YC-130A	2	C-130G	4	HC-130N	15
C-130A	202	C-130H	636	HC-130P	20
GC-130A	2	C-130H-MP	4	EC-130Q	18
RC-130A	15	C-130H-30	56	KC-130R	14
C-130B	156	HC-130H	68	LC-130R	6
HC-130B	12	HC-130H(N)	3	C-130T	12
WC-130B	5	HC-130H-7	10	KC-130T	22
C-130D	12	KC-130H	22	KC-130T-30	2
C-130E	486	LC-130H	4	AC-130U	12
EC-130E	1	MC-130H	24	L-100	22
C-130F	7	VC-130H	1	L-100-20	27
KC-130F	46	C-130J	1	L-100-30	67
LC-130F	4	C-130K	66	**Total**	**2086**

Note: The above quantities are based on Lockheed estimates for manufacture up to March 1994. However, production continues and the quantities quoted for models such as the C-130H are certain to increase.

APPENDIX B
TECHNICAL DATA FOR MAIN C-130 VARIANTS

LOCKHEED C-130A

Powerplants
Four Allison T56-A-9 turboprops, each rated at 3,750eshp

Dimensions and Weights
Wing span: 132ft 7in (40.41m)
Overall length: 97ft 9in (29.79m)
Height over tail: 38ft 3in (11.66m)
Wing area: 1,745sq ft (162.12sq m)
Operating weight: 61,842lb (28,051kg)
Maximum payload: 36,600lb (16,600kg)
Maximum normal take-off weight: 124,200lb (56,340kg)

Performance (at maximum take-off weight unless stated otherwise)
Maximum level speed: 383mph (616km/h)
Maximum cruising speed: 356mph (573km/h)
Sea level rate of climb: 1,700ft/min (518m/min)
Service ceiling at 100,000lb:34,000ft (10,360m)
Take-off to clear 50ft obstacle: 3,720ft (1,135m)
Landing from 50ft at 100,000lb: 2,600ft (792m)
Range with maximum payload: 1,830 miles (2,945 km)
Range with maximum fuel: 3,350 miles (5,390 km)

LOCKHEED C-130E

Powerplants
Four Allison T56-A-7 turboprops, each rated at 4,050eshp

Dimensions and Weights
Wing span: 132ft 7in (40.41m)
Overall length: 97ft 9in (29.79m)
Height over tail: 38ft 3in (11.66m)
Wing area: 1,745sq ft (162.12sq m)
Operating weight: 73,563lb (33,368kg)
Maximum payload: 45,579lb (20,674kg)
Maximum normal take-off weight: 155,000lb (70,308kg)

Performance (at maximum take-off weight unless stated otherwise)
Maximum level speed: 384mph (618km/h)
Maximum cruising speed: 368mph (592km/h)
Sea level rate of climb: 1,830ft/min (558m/min)
Service ceiling at 155,000lb: 23,000ft (7,010m)
Take-off to clear 50ft obstacle: 5,580ft (1,700m)
Landing from 50ft at 130,000lb: 3,750ft (1,143m)
Range with maximum payload and reserves: 2,420 miles (3,895 km)
Range with maximum fuel: 4,700 miles (7,560 km)

LOCKHEED C-130H

Powerplants
Four Allison T56-A-15 turboprops, each rated at 4,508eshp

Dimensions and Weights
Wing span: 132ft 7in (40.41m)
Overall length: 97ft 9in (29.79m)
Height over tail: 38ft 3in (11.66m)
Wing area: 1,745sq ft (162.12sq m)
Operating weight: 76,505lb (34,702kg)
Maximum payload: 42,637lb (19,340kg)
Maximum normal take-off weight: 155,000lb (70,308kg)
Design landing weight: 130,000lb (58,968kg)

Performance (at maximum take-off weight unless stated otherwise)
Maximum level speed: 385mph (620km/h)
Long range cruising speed: 332mph (535km/h)
Sea level rate of climb: 1,900ft/min (579m/min)
Service ceiling at 130,000lb: 33,000ft (10,060m)
Take-off to clear 50ft obstacle at 155,000lb: 5,160ft (1,573m)
Landing from 50ft at 100,000lb: 2,400ft (731m)
Range with maximum payload and reserves: 2,356 miles (3,791 km)
Range with maximum fuel: 4,894 miles (7,876 km)

LOCKHEED C-130J

Powerplants
Four Allison AE2100D3 turboprops, each rated at 4,591eshp

Dimensions and Weights
Wing span: 132ft 7in (40.41m)
Overall length: 97ft 9in (29.79m)
Height over tail: 38ft 3in (11.66m)
Wing area: 1,745sq ft (162.12sq m)
Operating weight: 79,090lb (35,875kg)
Maximum payload: 41,043lb (8,617kg)
Maximum normal take-off weight: 155,000lb (70,308kg)
Design landing weight: 130,000lb (58,968kg)

Performance (at maximum take-off weight unless stated otherwise)
Design cruise speed: 365mph (586km/h)
Sea level rate of climb: 2,234ft/min (681m/min)
Service ceiling at 100,000lb: 40,000ft
Range with maximum payload: 2,700 miles (4,563km)
Range with maximum fuel: 4,700 miles (7,943)

LOCKHEED L-100-30

Powerplants
Four Allison 501-D22A turboprops, each rated at 4,508eshp

Dimensions and Weights
Wing span: 132ft 7in (40.41m)
Overall length: 112ft 9in (34.37m)
Height over tail: 38ft 3in (11.66m)
Wing area: 1,745sq ft (162.12sq m)
Operating weight: 77,905lb (35,337kg)
Maximum payload: 50,885lb (23,081kg)
Maximum normal take-off weight: 155,000lb (70,308kg)

Performance (at maximum take-off weight unless stated otherwise)
Maximum cruising speed at 120,000lb: 363mph (583km/h)
Sea level rate of climb: 1,700ft/min (518m/min)
Take-off roll: 6,200ft (1,890m)
Landing from 50ft at 135,000lb: 4,850ft (1,478m)
Range with maximum payload and reserves: 1,569 miles (2,526m)
Range with zero payload and reserves: 5,733 miles (9,227 km)

APPENDIX C
NEW-BUILD AIRCRAFT – CONSTRUCTION NUMBERS

The following list details the production of new aircraft with individual airframes identified by their Lockheed constructor's number.

PROTOTYPES AND INITIAL PRODUCTION MODEL DERIVATIVES

YC-130A (2)	1001-1002
C-130A (204)	3001-3190, 3203-3216
C-130D (12)	3191-3202
RC-130A (15)	3217-3231

C-130B AND DERIVATIVES

C-130B (156)	3501-3528, 3530-3532, 3534-3541, 3543-3547, 3549-3553, 3556-3561, 3563, 3568-3572, 3575-3576, 3578-3591, 3593, 3596-3604, 3610-3618, 3620-3622, 3624-3626, 3628-3630, 3633-3635, 3637, 3639, 3642-3643, 3646-3649, 3652-3656, 3667-3679, 3682-3683, 3689-3692, 3697-3701, 3724, 3749-3751, 3764-3769, 3781
HC-130B (12)	3529, 3533, 3542, 3548, 3594-3595, 3638, 3641, 3650, 3745, 3763, 3773
WC-130B (5)	3702, 3707-3708, 3721-3722
C-130F (7)	3636, 3645, 3660, 3661, 3666, 3686, 3696
KC-130F (46)	3554-3555, 3566, 3573-3574, 3577, 3592, 3605-3608, 3619, 3623, 3627, 3631-3632, 3640, 3644, 3657-3658, 3664-3665, 3680, 3684-3685, 3693-3695, 3703-3705, 3709-3711, 3718-3719, 3723, 3725-3728, 3733-3734, 3740-3742
LC-130F (4)	3562, 3564-3565, 3567

C-130E AND DERIVATIVES

C-130E (486)	3609, 3651, 3659, 3662-3663, 3681, 3687-3688, 3706, 3712-3717, 3720, 3729-3732, 3735-3739, 3743-3744, 3746-3748, 3752-3762, 3770-3772, 3774-3780, 3782-3848, 3850-3857, 3859-3870, 3872-3877, 3879-3945, 3947-4035, 4039-4051, 4056-4071, 4074-4080, 4083, 4085-4087, 4090-4093, 4095-4096, 4100, 4105, 4113-4115, 4117-4119, 4122, 4124, 4128, 4136, 4148-4149, 4153-4154, 4159-4160, 4167-4168, 4171-4172, 4177-4178, 4180-4181, 4189-4194, 4202, 4215, 4276, 4282-4298, 4304, 4306-4311, 4314-4332, 4340-4349, 4351-4354, 4356-4357, 4359-4360, 4365, 4386-4387, 4389-4390, 4392-4394, 4398-4399, 4402, 4404, 4410, 4413-4415, 4417-4421, 4423-4429, 4434-4435, 4499-4500, 4502, 4504-4506, 4509-4510, 4514, 4517, 4519, 4521, 4524, 4527
EC-130E (1)	4158
C-130G (4)	3849, 3858, 3871, 3878

C-130H AND DERIVATIVES

C-130H (636)	4052-4054, 4312-4313, 4334-4339, 4366, 4369, 4373, 4395-4397, 4400-4401, 4403, 4405-4409, 4411, 4416, 4422, 4430-4433, 4436-4449, 4451-4471, 4473-4474, 4476, 4478-4498, 4515, 4518, 4520, 4523, 4525-4526, 4530-4531, 4533-4538, 4540-4557, 4559-4560, 4563-4564, 4566-4581, 4583-4585, 4587-4589, 4591-4592, 4594, 4596-4599, 4602-4605, 4607-4609, 4611-4614, 4616-4624, 4627-4628, 4630-4634, 4637-4641, 4643-4647, 4649-4651, 4653-4659, 4661-4663, 4665-4672, 4674-4675, 4678, 4680-4682, 4685-4688, 4690, 4692-4694, 4697, 4699-4700, 4703-4705, 4707, 4709, 4711, 4713-4714, 4716-4724, 4726-4730, 4732-4736, 4738-4745, 4747-4749, 4751-4756, 4758-4759, 4761, 4765-4767, 4769, 4771-4772, 4774-4775, 4777-4780, 4782-4795, 4797, 4801-4813, 4815, 4817-4823, 4825, 4827, 4829, 4831, 4835-4838, 4840-4846, 4848, 4852, 4854-4863, 4875-4879, 4881-4882, 4884-4885, 4887-4888, 4890, 4892, 4899-4900, 4902-4903, 4905-4906, 4908, 4910-4916, 4918, 4920, 4922, 4924, 4926, 4928-4930, 4934-4939, 4941-4946, 4948, 4964-4965, 4968, 4970-4971, 4973, 4975-4977, 4979-4980, 4982-4983, 4985, 4990-4991, 4994-4995, 4998, 5008, 5012, 5014-5015, 5017-5018, 5020-5021, 5038-5039, 5043-5044, 5046-5047, 5049-5052, 5058-5084, 5086, 5088-5090, 5093-5103, 5105, 5108-5114, 5116, 5119, 5122-5129, 5136-5138, 5141, 5154-5172, 5175, 5177-5183, 5185-5186, 5192-5201, 5203-5205, 5207, 5209, 5213-5218, 5220-5221, 5223, 5234-5235, 5238-5242, 5245-5254, 5267, 5269-5272, 5274, 5276, 5278-5279, 5282-5293, 5295-5297, 5308, 5310, 5312-5315, 5317-5318, 5321-5338, 5343, 5346-5355
C-130H-MP (4)	4847, 4849, 4866, 4898
C-130H-30 (56)	4864-4865, 4868-4870, 4894, 4897, 4919, 4921, 4925, 4927, 4933, 4959, 4961-4963, 4986-4987, 4989, 4997, 5001, 5003, 5006, 5019, 5030, 5036, 5140, 5142, 5144, 5146, 5148, 5150-5153, 5184, 5187, 5191, 5206, 5208, 5211-5212, 5224, 5226, 5227, 5264, 5268, 5273, 5275, 5277, 5280-5281, 5309, 5311, 5316, 5319
HC-130H (68)	4036-4038, 4055, 4072-4073, 4081-4082, 4084, 4088-4089, 4094, 4097-4099, 4102-4104, 4106-4108, 4110-4112, 4116, 4120-4121, 4123, 4125-4127, 4130-4133, 4135, 4138-4142, 4150-4151, 4255, 4260, 4265, 4501, 4507, 4513, 4528-4529, 4757, 4760, 4762, 4764, 4931, 5023, 5028, 5031, 5033-5035, 5037, 5104, 5106-5107, 5120-5121
HC-130H(N) (3)	5202, 5210, 5294
HC-130H-7 (10)	4947, 4958, 4966-4967, 4969, 4993, 4996, 4999, 5002, 5005
KC-130H (22)	4503, 4511, 4532, 4539, 4625, 4636, 4642,

	4648, 4652, 4660, 4664, 4746, 4750, 4814, 4816, 4871-4874, 4907, 4909, 4940
LC-130H (4)	5007, 5010, 5013, 5016
MC-130H (24)	5004, 5026, 5041-5042, 5053-5054, 5091-5092, 5115, 5117-5118, 5130-5135, 5173, 5236-5237, 5243-5244, 5265-5266
VC-130H (1)	4737
C-130K (66)	4169, 4182, 4188, 4195-4196, 4198-4201, 4203-4207, 4210-4214, 4216-4220, 4223-4224, 4226-4228, 4230-4233, 4235-4238, 4240-4247, 4251-4254, 4256-4259, 4261-4264, 4266-4268, 4270-4275
HC-130N (15)	4363, 4367-4368, 4370-4372, 4374-4382
HC-130P (20)	4143, 4152, 4155-4157, 4161-4166, 4173-4175, 4179, 4183-4187
EC-130Q (18)	4239, 4249, 4269, 4277-4281, 4595, 4601, 4781, 4867, 4896, 4901, 4904, 4932, 4984, 4988
KC-130R (14)	4615, 4626, 4629, 4635, 4677, 4683, 4689, 4696, 4702, 4712, 4768, 4770, 4773, 4776
LC-130R (6)	4305, 4508, 4516, 4522, 4725, 4731
C-130T (12)	5255, 5258, 5298-5301, 5304-5305, 5341-5342, 5344-5345
KC-130T (22)	4972, 4974, 4978, 4981, 5009, 5011, 5040, 5045, 5085, 5087, 5143, 5145, 5147, 5149, 5174, 5176, 5219, 5222, 5302-5303, 5339-5340
KC-130T-30 (2)	5260, 5263
AC-130U (12)	5139, 5228-5233, 5256-5257, 5259, 5261-5262

C-130J

C-130J (1)	5408

LOCKHEED L–100 COMMERCIAL DERIVATIVES

L–100 (22)	3946, 4101, 4109, 4129, 4134, 4137, 4144-4147 4170, 4176, 4197, 4208-4209, 4221-4222, 4225, 4229, 4234, 4248, 4250
L–100-20 (27)	4299-4303, 4333, 4350, 4355, 4358, 4361-4362, 4364, 4383-4385, 4412, 4450, 4512, 4593, 4706, 4708, 4710, 4715, 4830, 4832, 4850, 4853
L–100-30 (67)	4388, 4391, 4472, 4475, 4477, 4558, 4561-4562, 4565, 4582, 4586, 4590, 4600, 4606, 4610, 4673, 4676, 4679, 4684, 4691, 4695, 4698, 4701, 4763, 4796, 4798-4800, 4824, 4826, 4828, 4833-4834, 4839, 4851, 4880, 4883, 4886, 4889, 4891, 4893, 4895, 4917, 4923, 4949-4957, 4960, 4992, 5000, 5022, 5024-5025, 5027, 5029, 5032, 5048, 5225, 5306-5307, 5320

UNUSED CONSTRUCTION NUMBERS

Aircraft not built (3)	5055-5057

Note: Quite why these numbers were unused is not clear and it is possible that they may exist, for example, c/n 5048 is listed as unbuilt, even though there have been reports of an L-100-30 with the American civil registration N82178 carrying this construction number on its manufacturer's identity plate which describes it as an L.382G-44K-30.

The C-130 production line at Lockheed Aeronautical Systems Company, Marietta. In the foreground is C-130H (81-0629) that was destined to remain on the airfield for the USAF Reserve squadron at Dobbins AFB.

APPENDIX D
C–130 POST–PRODUCTION MODIFICATION LIST

The following list details the modification of C–130s between variants after initial manufacture. Individual airframes are identified by constructor's number.

From YC-130
to NC-130: 1001, 1002

From C-130A
to C-130A-II: 3092, 3132-3133, 3136, 3138, 3142-3143, 3145-3146, 3148-3149
to AC-130A: 3010, 3013, 3038, 3041, 3056, 3067, 3070-3071, 3073, 3077, 3117
to DC-130A: 3099, 3122, 3135, 3168, 3203-3204
to GC-130A: 3008, 3064, 3125, 3147, 3178
to JC-130A: 3001-3007, 3012, 3014-3017, 3026, 3098, 3101, 3105
to NC-130A: 3009, 3022, 3049-3050
to TC-130A: 3019
to C-130D: 3048, 3180-3181

From C-130A-II
to C-130A: 3092, 3132-3133, 3138, 3142-3143, 3145-3146, 3148-3149

From DC-130A
to C-130A: 3135, 3168

From JC-130A
to C-130A: 3004, 3006-3007, 3026
to AC-130A: 3001, 3012, 3014-3017, 3098
to GC-130A: 3003
to NC-130A: 3005
to RC-130S: 3101, 3105

From NC-130A
to C-130A: 3022, 3050

From RC-130A
to C-130A: 3019, 3217-3229, 3231
to DC-130A: 3230

From RC-130S
to C-130A: 3101, 3105

Originally built as a C-130E (69-6569 c/n 4343) this aircraft was subsequently modified to an AC-130E and more recently to AC-130H standard.

From TC-130A
to RC-130A: 3019

From C-130B
to C-130B-II: 3506, 3518, 3560-3561, 3563, 3568, 3571, 3576, 3579, 3581, 3585-3586, 3589
to GC-130B: 3522, 3537
to JC-130B: 3501-3505, 3508-3512, 3549, 3557, 3647-3648
to KC-130B: 3519, 3557, 3611, 3615-3616, 3620
to NC-130B: 3507
to WC-130B: 3520-3521, 3524, 3526, 3528, 3530, 3537-3538, 3545, 3551, 3559

From C-130B-II
to C-130B: 3506, 3518, 3560-3561, 3563, 3568, 3571, 3576, 3579, 3581, 3585-3586, 3589

From JC-130B
to C-130B: 3501-3505, 3508-3509, 3511, 3549, 3557, 3647-3648
to NC-130B: 3512
to VC-130B: 3510

From NC-130B
to C-130B: 3512

From VC-130B
to C-130B: 3510

From WC-130B
to C-130B: 3520-3521, 3524, 3528, 3530, 3537-3538, 3545, 3551, 3359, 3702, 3707-3708, 3721-3722

From C-130D
to C-130A: 3180-3181
to DC-130A: 3048
to C-130D-6: 3191-3196
to GC-130D: 3197

From C-130D-6
to GC-130D-6: 3193, 3196

From C-130E
to C-130E-I: 3806, 3852, 3992, 4007*, 4040, 4046*, 4056*, 4059, 4062*, 4065*, 4068*, 4071, 4074*, 4077*, 4080*, 4083*, 4086* (* also known as C-130H(CT)
to C-130E-II: 3770, 3777, 3780, 3783, 3788, 3795, 3799, 3821, 3827
to AC-130E: 4341-4349, 4351-4352

This EC-130E(RR) 63-7783 c/n 3850 was manufactured as a C-130E, entered service as an EC-130E(CL) and was later modified to EC-130E(RR). PHOTO: PETER R. MARCH

to DC-130E: 3662-3663, 3681, 3687, 3713-3714, 3716
to EC-130E(CL): 3850, 3889, 3894, 3896, 3977
to EC-130E(RR): 3839, 3939, 3978
to JC-130E: 3609
to NC-130E: 4087, 4090
to WC-130E: 3659, 3688, 3706, 4047-4049

From C-130E-I
to MC-130E(C): 4007,4046, 4056, 4062, 4065, 4068, 4080, 4083, 4086, 4090
to MC-130E(Y): 3806, 3852, 4074, 4077

From C-130E-II
to EC-130E(ABCCC): 3738, 3770, 3780, 3783, 3795, 3799, 3821, 3827

From AC-130E
to AC-130H: 4341-4344, 4346-4349, 4351-4352

From DC-130E
to C-130E: 3662-3663, 3681, 3687, 3713-3714, 3716

From EC-130E(ABCCC)
to C-130E: 3783

From EC-130E(CL)
to EC-130E(RR): 3850

From JC-130E
to C-130E: 3609

From MC-130E(S)
to MC-130E(Y): 4087

From NC-130E
to C-130E-I: 4090
to MC-130E(S): 4087

From C-130G
to EC-130G: 3849, 3858, 3871, 3878

From EC-130G
to TC-130G: 3849, 3858, 3878

From C-130H
to EC-130H: 4542-4543, 4545-4550, 4554, 4557, 4563-4564
to EC-130H(CL): 4735, 5194
to VC-130H: 4605, 4803, 4811
to YMC-130H: 4669

From DC-130H
to NC-130H: 4131

From HC-130H
to C-130H: 4255, 4260, 4265
to DC-130H: 4131
to EC-130H: 4082, 4089, 4102, 4150
to JC-130H: 4081
to JHC-130H: 4038, 4073
to NC-130H: 4116

to WC-130H:	4088, 4099, 4103-4104, 4106-4108, 4110-4111, 4120, 4126-4127, 4132, 4139-4140
to HC-130P:	4037-4038, 4072, 4081, 4084, 4094, 4097-4098, 4116, 4121, 4125, 4130, 4142
to EC-130V:	5121
From JC-130H	
to HC-130H:	4081
From JHC-130H	
to NC-130H:	4038, 4073
From NC-130H	
to HC-130H:	4038, 4073, 4116
From WC-130H	
to C-130H:	4099, 4104, 4108, 4111, 4120, 4126-4127, 4140
From EC-130Q	
to TC-130Q:	4239, 4278, 4601
From C–130K–C1	
to C–130K–C1K:	4212, 4224, 4227, 4228, 4240, 4262
to C–130K–C1P:	4188, 4195, 4198-4199, 4203-4205, 4211, 4216-4217, 4223, 4230-4231, 4236-4237, 4242, 4245, 4256-4258, 4261, 4263-4264, 4267, 4274
to C–130K–W2:	4233
to C–130K–C3P:	4169, 4182, 4200-4201, 4206-4207, 4210, 4213, 4218, 4220, 4226, 4232, 4235, 4238, 4241, 4244, 4246-4247, 4251-4254, 4259, 4266, 4268, 4270-4273, 4275
From C–130K–C1K	
to C–130K–C1P:	4212
From L–100	
to L–100-20:	3946, 4129, 4147, 4170, 4176, 4221-4222, 4225, 4250
to L–100-30:	4101, 4134, 4208, 4248
From L–100-20	
to L–100-30:	4147, 4222, 4225, 4299-4301, 4333, 4383-4384
to L–100–HTTB:	4412

Thirty of the RAF's C-130Ks were 'stretched' by 15ft and were designated Hercules C3s in service. PHOTO: PETER R. MARCH

APPENDIX E
NEW-BUILD AIRCRAFT – SERIALS & REGISTRATIONS

The following listing includes details of aircraft by serial number or civil registration, together with the appropriate Lockheed construction number and customer at delivery.

YC-130

US Air Force (2)

53-3396 to 53-3397   1001-1002

C-130A

US Air Force (190)

53-3129 to 53-3135   3001-3007
54-1621 to 54-1640   3008-3027
55-0001 to 55-0048   3028-3075
56-0468 to 56-0551   3076-3159
57-0453 to 57-0483   3160-3190

Australia (12)

A97-205 to A97-216   3205-3216

GC-130A (later DC-130A)

US Air Force (2)

57-0496 to 57-0497   3203-3204

RC-130A

US Air Force (15)

57-0510 to 57-0524   3217-3231

C-130B

US Air Force (128)

57-0525 to 57-0529   3501-3505
58-0711 to 58-0758   3506-3528,3530-3532, 3534-3541, 3543-3547, 3549-3553, 3556-3559
59-1524 to 59-1537   3560-3561, 3563, 3568, 3571, 3569, 3576, 3579, 3581, 3586, 3570, 3585, 3588-3589
59-5957   3584
60-0293 to 60-0310   3591, 3593, 3596-3597, 3600, 3602-3604, 3610-3611, 3613, 3612, 3614, 3617-3618, 3620-3622
61-0948 to 61-0972   3624-3626, 3628-3630, 3633-3635, 3637, 3639, 3642-3643, 3646-3649, 3652-3656, 3667-3669
61-2634 to 61-2649   3670-3679, 3682-3683, 3689-3692
62-3487   3697

Canada (4)

10301 to 10304   3572, 3575, 3587, 3590

Indonesia (9)

T1302 to T1310   3578, 3580, 3582-3583, 3598-3599, 3601, 3615-3616

Iran (4)

5-101 to 5-104   3698-3701

Pakistan (4)

24140 to 24143   3751, 3766, 3768, 3781

South Africa (7)

401 to 407   3724, 3749-3750, 3764-3765, 3767, 3769

HC-130B

US Coast Guard (12)

1339 to 1342   3529, 3533, 3542, 3548
1344 to 1351   3594-3595, 3638, 3641, 3650, 3745, 3763, 3773

WC-130B

US Air Force (5)

62-3492 to 62-3496   3702, 3707-3708, 3721-3722

C-130D

US Air Force (12)

57-0484 to 57-0495   3191-3202

C-130E

US Air Force (390)

61-2358 to 61-2373   3609, 3651, 3659, 3662-3663, 3681, 3687-3688, 3706, 3712-3717, 3720
62-1784 to 62-1866   3729-3732, 3735-3739, 3743-3744, 3746-3748, 3752-3762, 3770-3772, 3774-3780, 3782-3812, 3814-3830
63-7764 to 63-7899   3813, 3831-3848, 3850-3857, 3859-3860, 3872-3873, 3861-3870, 3874-3877, 3879-3883, 3888-3889, 3894-3895, 3884-3887, 3890-3893, 3903-3904, 3896-3902, 3905-3945, 3947-3970
63-9810 to 63-9817   3971-3978
64-0495 to 64-0572   3979-4010, 4013-4014, 4017-4019, 4021-4025, 4027-4035, 4039-4040, 4043-4049, 4056-4059, 4062-4063, 4065, 4068, 4071, 4074, 4077, 4080, 4083, 4086, 4079, 4085, 4087, 4090
64-17680 to 64-17681   4064, 4069
64-18240   4105
68-10934 to 68-10951   4314-4331
69-6566 to 69-6583   4340-4349, 4351-4354, 4356-4357, 4359-4360
70-1259 to 70-1276   4404, 4410, 4413-4415, 4417-4421, 4423-4426, 4428-4429, 4434-4435
72-1288 to 72-1299   4499-4500, 4502, 4504-4506, 4509-4510, 4517, 4519, 4521, 4527

Argentina (3)

TC-61 to TC-63   4308-4310

Australia (12)

A97-159 to A97-160   4159-4160
A97-167 to A97-168   4167-4168
A97-171 to A97-172   4171-4172
A97-177 to A97-178   4177-4178
A97-180 to A97-181   4180-4181
A97-189 to A97-190   4189-4190

Brazil (11)

2450 to 2460   4091-4093, 4113-4114, 4202, 4287, 4290-4293

Canada (24)

130305 to 130328   4020, 4026, 4041-4042, 4050-4051, 4060-4061, 4066-4067, 4070, 4075, 4122, 4124, 4095-4096, 4191-4194, 4285-4286, 4288-4289

Iran (28)

5-105 to 5-132   4115, 4117-4119, 4148-4149, 4153-4154, 4276, 4282-4284, 4294-4298, 4365, 4386-4387, 4389-4390, 4392-4394, 4398-4399, 4402

Saudi Arabia (9)

451 to 455   4076, 4078, 4128, 4136, 4215

The NC-130B, after storage, was converted for a new role with NASA for Earth Survey.

1606 to 1609	4304, 4306-4307, 4311
Sweden (1)	
84002	4332
Turkey (8)	
13186 to 13189	4011-4012, 4015-4016
17949	4100
01947	4427
11468	4514
30991	4524

EC-130E

US Coast Guard (1)	
1414	4158

C-130F

US Navy (7)	
149787	3636
149790	3645
149793 to 149794	3660-3661
149797	3666
149801	3686
149805	3696

KC-130F

US Marine Corps (46)	
147572 to 147573	3554-3555
148246 to 148249	3566, 3573-3574, 3577
148890 to 148899	3592, 3605-3608, 3619, 3623, 3627, 3631-3632
149788 to 149789	3640, 3644
149791 to 149792	3657-3658
149795 to 149796	3664-3665
149798 to 149800	3680, 3684-3685
149802 to 149804	3693-3695
149806 to 149816	3703-3705, 3709-3711, 3718-3719, 3723, 3725-3726
150684 to 150690	3727-3728, 3733-3734, 3740-3742

LC-130F

US Navy (4)	
148318 to 148321	3562, 3564-3565, 3567

C-130G

US Navy (4)	
151888 to 151891	3849, 3858, 3871, 3878

C-130H

US Air Force (257)	
73-1580 to 73-1588	4542-4550
73-1590	4554
73-1592	4557
73-1594 to 73-1595	4563-4564
73-1597 to 73-1598	4570, 4573
74-1658 to 74-1693	4579, 4585, 4592, 4596-4598, 4603-4604, 4611, 4613, 4616-4617, 4620-4621, 4623, 4627, 4631, 4640-4641, 4643, 4645-4646, 4651, 4654, 4657-4658, 4663, 4666, 4669-4670, 4675, 4681-4682, 4687-4688, 4693

74-2061 to 74-2072	4644, 4647, 4655, 4659, 4667, 4671, 4678, 4694, 4699-4700, 4703, 4705
74-2130 to 74-2134	4711, 4718, 4722, 4730, 4735
78-0806 to 78-0813	4815, 4817-4823
79-0473 to 79-0480	4852, 4854-4860
80-0320 to 80-0326	4900, 4902-4903, 4905-4906, 4908, 4910
80-0332	4943
81-0626 to 81-0631	4939, 4941-4942, 4944-4946
82-0054 to 82-0061	4968,4970-4971, 4973, 4975, 4977, 4979, 4982
83-0486 to 83-0489	5008, 5012, 5014, 5018
84-0204 to 84-0213	5038-5039, 5043-5044, 5046-5047, 5049-5052
85-0035 to 85-0042	5073-5074, 5077, 5079-5080, 5083, 5086, 5089
85-1361 to 85-1368	5071-5072, 5075-5076, 5078, 5081-5082, 5084
86-0410 to 86-0415	5094, 5097-5098, 5100, 5102, 5105
86-0418 to 86-0419	5110, 5113
86-1391 to 86-1398	5093, 5095-5096, 5099, 5101, 5103, 5111-5112
87-9281 to 87-9288	5122-5129
88-1301 to 88-1308	5162-5169
88-4401 to 88-4408	5154-5161
89-1051 to 89-1056	5198-5199, 5201, 5203-5205
89-1181 to 89-1188	5188, 5190, 5192-5197
89-9101 to 89-9106	5216-5218, 5220-5221, 5223
90-1057 to 90-1058	5240-5241
90-1791 to 90-1798	5242, 5245-5251
90-9107 to 90-9108	5238-5239
91-1231 to 91-1239	5278, 5282-5289
91-1651 to 91-1653	5290-5292
91-9141 to 91-9144	5293, 5295-5297
(not yet allocated)	5279, 5310, 5312-5315, 5321-5338, 5343, 5348-5355

Abu Dhabi (now UAE) (6)

1211 to 1212	4580, 4584
1211 to 1214	4983, 4985, 4879, 4882

Note: Duplication of serial numbers is explained by the fact that the first two aircraft listed were disposed of, and their identities re-used.

Algeria (10)

7T-WHE to 7T-WHF	4935, 4934
7T-WHI to 7T-WHJ	4930, 4928
7T-WHQ to 7T-WHT	4926, 4924, 4912, 4911
7T-WHY to 7T-WHZ	4913, 4914

Argentina (5)

TC-64 to TC-68	4436-4437, 4464, 4576, 4578

Australia (12)

A97-001 to A97-012	4780, 4782-4791, 4793

Belgium (12)

CH-01 to CH-12	4455, 4460-4461, 4467, 4470, 4473, 4476, 4478-4479, 4481-4483

Bolivia (2)

TAM-90 to TAM-91	4744, 4759

Brazil (6)

2463 to 2468	4570, 4602, 4630, 4990-4991, 4998

Cameroon (2)

TJX-AC	4747
TJX-AD	4752

Canada (12)

130329 to 130335	4553, 4555, 4559, 4568, 4574, 4994-4995
130338 to 130342	5175, 5177, 5189, 5200, 5207

Note: Aircraft 130336 and 130337 were obtained second-hand, after service with Abu Dhabi.

Chad (1)

TT-PAF	5141

Chile (2)

995 to 996	4453, 4496

Colombia (2)

1001	4964
1005	4965

Denmark (3)

B-678 to B-680	4572, 4587, 4599

Ecuador (3)

743	4743
748	4748
812	4812

Egypt (23)

1270 to 1292	4707, 4709, 4714, 4719, 4721, 4728, 4792, 4794-4795, 4797, 4802-4811, 4936-4938

France (3) Construction numbers are also used as serial numbers.

5114	5114
5116	5116
5119	5119

Gabon (1)

TR-KKC	4765

Greece (12)

741 to 752	4622, 4632, 4665, 4672, 4716, 4720, 4723-4724, 4727, 4729, 4732, 4734

Indonesia (3)

A-1315 to A-1316	4838, 4840
A-1323	4899

Iran (32)

5-133 to 5-162	4432-4433, 4438-4440, 4442, 4444-4445, 4448, 4454, 4456-4459, 4462-4463, 4465-4466, 4468-4469, 4471, 4474, 4480, 4484-4490
5-157 to 5-158	4591, 4594

Note: The final two aircraft were acquired after earlier machines were renumbered to eliminate 'gaps' caused by attrition losses.

Israel (10)

4X-JUA/02	4430
4X-JUB/06	4431
4X-FBC/009	4530
4X-FBD/011	4533
4X-FBQ/420	4653
4X-FBS/427	4662
4X-FBT/435	4668
4X-FBU/448	4680
4X-FBW/436	4686
4X-FBX/428	4692

Italy (14)

MM61988 to MM62001	4441, 4443, 4446-4447, 4449, 4451-4452, 4491-4495, 4497-4498

Japan (15)

35-1071 to 35-1072	4976, 4980
45-1073 to 45-1074	5015, 5017
65-1075 to 65-1076	5088, 5090
75-1077 to 75-1078	5108-5109
85-1079 to 85-1080	5136, 5138
95-1081 to 95-1083	5170-5172
05-1084 to 05-1085	5213-5214

Jordan (4)

144	4779
345 to 347	4813, 4920, 4929

Libya (16)

111 to 118	4366, 4369, 4373, 4395, 4400-4401, 4403, 4405
119 to 124	4515, 4518, 4523, 4525, 4536, 4538

126 to 127 — 4541, 4540

Note: Aircraft 119-124 and 126-127 not delivered due to embargo.

Malaysia (6)

FM2401 to FM2406 — 4656, 4661, 4674, 4685, 4690, 4697

Morocco (17) Construction numbers are also used as serial numbers.

CNA-OA to CNA-OQ — 4535, 4537, 4551, 4575, 4581, 4583, 4713, 4717, 4733, 4738-4739, 4742, 4875-4877, 4888, 4892

New Zealand (5)

NZ7001 to NZ7005 — 4052-4054, 4312-4313

Niger (2)

5U-MBD — 4829

5U-MBH — 4831

Nigeria (6)

910 to 915 — 4619, 4624, 4638-4639, 4649-4650

Norway (6)

952 to 957 — 4334-4339

Oman (3)

501 to 503 — 4878, 4916, 4948

The Philippines (3) Construction numbers are also used as serial numbers.

4704 — 4704

4726 — 4726

4761 — 4761

Portugal (5)

6801 to 6805 — 4749, 4753, 4772, 4777-4778

Saudi Arabia (38)

102 — 4605

460 to 470 — 4566-4567, 4637, 4607-4609, 4740-4741, 4751, 4754, 4756

472 to 475 — 5234-5235, 5252-5253

1601 to 1605 — 4612, 4614, 4618, 4633-4634

1610 to 1612 — 4396-4397, 4552

1614 to 1615 — 4560, 4745

1618 to 1619 — 4755, 4758

1623 to 1626 — 5254, 5267, 5269-5270

HZ-116 — 4915

HZ-HM5 to HZ-HM6 — 4843, 4845

Singapore (5)

730 to 733 — 4842, 4844, 4846, 4848

735 — 5070

South Korea (8) Construction numbers are also used as serial numbers.

5178 to 5183 — 5178-5183

5185 to 5186 — 5185-5186

Spain (7)

T.10-1 to T.10-4 — 4520, 4526, 4531, 4534

T.10-8 to T.10-10 — 4835-4836, 4841

Sudan (6)

1100 to 1105 — 4766-4767, 4769, 4771, 4774-4775

Sweden (6)

84003 to 84008 — 4628, 4881, 4884-4885, 4887, 4890

Taiwan (13)

1301 to 1312 — 5058-5069

1351 — 5215

Thailand (6)

60101 to 60103 — 4861-4863

60108 to 60110 — 5209, 5272, 5274

Tunisia (2)

TS-MTA to TS-MTB — 5020, 5021

Venezuela (8)

2716 — 5137

3134 — 4801

3556 — 4406

4224 — 4556

4951 — 4407

5320 — 4577

7772 — 4408

9508 — 4409

Yemen (2)

1150 — 4825

1160 — 4827

Zaire (7)

9T-TCA to 9T-TCB — 4411, 4416

9T-TCD to 9T-TCF — 4422, 4569, 4588

9T-TCG — 4589 (renumbered as 9T-TCC), 4736

Note: The final aircraft listed adopted the identity made vacant after renumbering the original 9T-TCG as 9T-TCC.

Unsold Aircraft (7)

(Identities not known) — 5271, 5276, 5308, 5317-5318, 5346-5347

C–130H(AEH)

Saudi Arabia (3)

HZ-MS07 — 4922

HZ-MS019 — 4837

HZ-MS021 — 4918

C-130H-MP

Indonesia (1)

A-1322 — 4898

Malaysia (3)

FM2451 to FM2453 — 4847, 4849, 4866

C-130H-30

Algeria (8)

7T-VHM to 7T-VHP — 4919, 4894, 4897, 4921

7T-WHA to 7T-WHB — 4997, 5224

7T-WHD — 4987

7T-WHL — 4989

Cameroon (1)

TJX-AE — 4933

Chad (1)

TT-AAH — 5184

Dubai (1)

312 — 4961

Egypt (3)

1293 to 1295 — 5187, 5191, 5206

France (9) Construction numbers are used as serial numbers.

5140 — 5140

5142 — 5142

5144 — 5144

5150 to 5153 — 5150-5153

5226 to 5227 — 5226-5227

Indonesia (7)

A-1317 to A-1321 — 4864-4865, 4868-4869, 4925

A-1324 — 4927

A-1331 — 4870

Malaysia (1)

M30-10 — 5268

Netherlands (2)

G-273 — 5273

G-275 — 5275

Nigeria (3)

916 to 918 — 4962-4963, 5001

Portugal (1)

6806 — 5264

Saudi Arabia (3)

471 — 5211

1622 — 5212

HZ-MS08 — 4986

South Korea (4) Construction numbers are used as serial numbers

5006 — 5006

Indonesian Air Force C-130H-30.

5019 5019
5030 5030
5036 5036
Spain (1)
TL.10-01 5003
Thailand (6)
60104 to 60107 4959, 5146, 5148, 5208
60111 to 60112 5280-5281
Unsold Aircraft (7)
(Identities not known) 5277, 5309, 5311, 5316, 5319

HC-130H
US Air Force (43)
64-14852 to 64-14866 4036-4038, 4055, 4072-4073, 4081-4082, 4084, 4088-4089, 4094, 4097-4099
65-0962 to 65-0987 4102-4104, 4106-4108, 4110-4112, 4116, 4120-4121, 4123, 4125-4127, 4130-4133, 4135, 4138-4142
65-0989 to 65-0990 4150-4151
US Coast Guard (25)
1452 to 1454 4255, 4260, 4265
1500 to 1504 4501, 4507, 4513, 4528-4529
1600 to 1603 4757, 4760, 4762, 4764
1710 to 1721 5028, 5031, 5033-5035, 5037, 5023, 5104, 5106-5107, 5120-5121
1790 4931

HC-130H(N)
US Air Force (3)
88-2101 to 88-2102 5202, 5210
91-2103 5294

HC-130H-7
US Coast Guard (10)
1700 to 1709 4947, 4958, 4966-4967, 4969, 4993, 4996, 4999, 5002, 5005

KC-130H
Argentina (2)
TC-69 to TC-70 4814, 4816
Brazil (2)
2461 to 2462 4625, 4636
Israel (2)
4X-FBY/522 4660
4X-FBZ/545 4664
Morocco (2) Construction numbers are also used as serial numbers.
CNA-OR to CNA-OS 4907, 4909
Saudi Arabia (8)
456 to 459 4503, 4511, 4532, 5439
1616 to 1617 4746, 4750
1620 to 1621 4872-4873
Singapore (1)
734 4940
Spain (5)
TK.10-5 to TK.10-7 4642, 4648, 4652
TK.10-11 to TK.10-12 4871, 4874

LC-130H
US Air Force (4)
83-0490 to 83-0493 5007, 5010, 5013, 5016

MC-130H
US Air Force (24)
83-1212 5004
84-0475 to 84-0476 5041-5042
85-0011 to 85-0012 5053-5054
86-1699 5026
87-0023 to 87-0024 5091-5092
87-0125 to 87-0127 5115, 5117-5118
88-0191 to 88-0195 5130-5134
88-0264 5135
88-1803 5173
89-0280 to 89-0283 5236-5237, 5243-5244
90-0161 to 90-0162 5265-5266

VC-130H
Saudi Arabia (1)
112 4737

C-130J
Prototype (1)
(Identity not known) 5408

C-130K
United Kingdom (66)
XV176 to XV223 4169, 4182, 4188, 4195-4196, 4198-4201, 4203-4207, 4210-4214, 4216-4220, 4223-4224, 4226-4228, 4230-4233, 4235-4238, 4240-4247, 4251-4253
XV290 to XV307 4254, 4256-4259, 4261-4264, 4266-4268, 4270-4275

HC-130N
US Air Force (15)

69-5819 to 69-5833	4363, 4367-4368, 4370-4372, 4374-4382

HC-130P
US Air Force (20)

65-0988	4143
65-0991 to 65-0994	4152, 4155-4157
66-0211 to 66-0225	4161-4166, 4173-4175, 4179, 4183-4187

EC-130Q
US Navy (18)

156170 to 156177	4239, 4249, 4269, 4277-4281
159348	4601
159469	4595
160608	4781
161223	4867
161494 to 161496	4896, 4901, 4904
161531	4932
162312 to 162313	4984, 4988

KC-130R
US Marine Corps (14)

160013 to 160021	4615, 4626, 4629, 4635, 4677, 4683, 4689, 4696, 4702
160240	4712
160625 to 160628	4768, 4770, 4773, 4776

LC-130R
US Navy (6)

155917	4305
159129 to 159131	4508, 4516, 4522
160740 to 160741	4725, 4731

C-130T
US Navy (12)

164762 to 164763	5255, 5258
164993 to 164998	5298-5301, 5304-5305
(Identity not known)	5341-5342, 5344-5345

KC-130T
US Marine Corps (22)

162308 to 162311	4972, 4974, 4978, 4981
162785 to 162786	5009, 5011
163022 to 163023	5040, 5045
163310 to 163311	5085, 5087
163591 to 163592	5143, 5145
164105 to 164106	5147, 5149
164180 to 164181	5174, 5176
164441 to 164442	5219, 5222
164759 to 164760	5302-5303
(Identity not known)	5339-5340

KC-130T-30
US Marine Corps (2)

164597 to 164598	5260, 5263

AC-130U
US Air Force (12)

87-0128	5139
89-0510 to 89-0515	5228-5233
90-0163 to 90-0167	5256-5257, 5259, 5261-5262

LOCKHEED L–100

Registration letters	*Constructor's Numbers*
Airlift International Inc. (3)	
N759AL, N760AL	4225, 4229
N9254R	4222
Alaska Airlines (3)	
N9227R	4208
N9248R	4221*
N9267R	4146*
Continental Air Services (2)	
N9260R, N9261R	4101*, 4109*
Delta Airlines (3)	
N9258R, N9259R	4170, 4176
N9268R	4147
International Aerodyne (1)	
N9262R	4248
Lockheed (1)	
N1130E	3946
National Aircraft Leasing (2)	
N7999S, N9266R	4234, 4250
Pacific Western Airlines (2)	
CF-PWO	4197
N9263R	4134*
Pakistan International Airlines (2)	
AP-AUT, AP-AUU	4144, 4145
Zambian Air Cargo (2)	
9J-RBW, 9J-RBX	4129, 4137
Zambian Government (1)	
9J-REZ	4209

LOCKHEED L–100-20

Air America (1)	
N7951S	4301 (for Southern Air Transport)
First National Bank of Chicago (1)	
N9265R	4300 (for Interior Airways)
Flying W Airways (2)	
N60FW, N70FW	4358, 4364
Gabon (1)	
TR-KKB	4710
Girard Trust (2)	
N7952S, N9237R	4302, 4303 (for Flying W Airways)
Kuwait (2)	
317, 318	4350, 4412
National Aircraft Leasing/Maple Leaf Leasing (1)	
N7960S	4355
Pacific Western Airlines (1)	
CF-PWX	4361
Peru (6)	
382 to 384	4706, 4708, 4715
396 to 398	4450, 4850, 4853
Philippine Government (2)	
RP-C100, RP-C101	4512, 4593
Safmarine (1)	
ZS-GSK	4385
Saturn Airways (3)	
N10ST, N11ST	4383, 4384
N7957S	4333*
Southern Air Transport (2)	
N7984S, N9232R	4362, 4299
TAAG-Angola Airlines (2)	
D2-EAS, D2–THA	4830, 4832

LOCKHEED L–100-30

AFI International (2)	
N4248M, N4269M	4992, 5000
Advanced Leasing Corporation (1)	
N82178	5048 (see footnote)
Air Algerie (3)	
7T-VHG	4880
7T-VHK, 7T-VHL	4883, 4886

Air Gabon (1)
TR-LBV 5024
Alaska International Air (2)
N108AK, N501AK 4763, 4798
China Air Cargo (2)
B-3002, B–3004 5025, 5027
Dubai (now UAE) (1)
311 4834
Ecuador (1)
893 4893
Ethiopian Airlines (3)
ET-AJK, ET–AJL 5022, 5029
ET-AKG 5306
Frameair (2)
PJ-TAC 5225
5307 (not sold)
Gabon (2)
TR-KKA, TR–KKD 4582, 4895
Indonesia (1)
A-1314 4800
Indonesian Government (3)
PK-PLR to PK-PLT 4889, 4917, 4923
Kuwait (4)
322 to 325 4949, 4951, 4953, 4955
Lockheed (2)
N4110M 4839 (for Wirtschaftsflug)
N4170M 4891 (for LADE)
Mitsui Corporation (3)
PK-PLU to PK-PLW 4824, 4826, 4828 (for Indonesian Govt)
Pacific Western Airlines (1)
C-GHPW 4799
Pemex (1)
XC-EXP 4851
Safair Freighters (17)
ZS-JIV to ZS-JIZ 4673, 4679, 4684, 4691, 4695
ZS-JJA 4698
ZS-JVL, ZS–JVM 4676, 4701
ZS-RSB to ZS-RSJ 4472, 4475, 4477, 4558, 4562, 4565, 4590, 4600, 4606
Saturn Airways (4)
N12ST, N15ST 4388, 4391
N20ST, N21ST 4561, 4586
Saudi Arabia (6)
HZ-117 4954
HZ-MS05, HZ-MS06 4950, 4952
HZ-MS09, HZ-MS10 4956, 4957
HS-MS14 4960
SCIBE Zaire (1)
9Q-CBJ 4796*
Transporte Aereo Boliviano (1)
CP-1564/TAM-92 4833 (for Bolivian Government)
Uganda Airlines (1)
5X-UCF 4610
Worldwide Trading (1)
N4281M 5032
Unsold Aircraft (1)
– 5320
* = denotes a leased aircraft

Angola Airlines L-100-20 sets off on its delivery flight.

APPENDIX F: MILITARY OPERATORS OF THE C–130/L–100 HERCULES

ABU DHABI/UAE

Unit	Type
C-130 Squadron, Bateen AB	C-130H

ALGERIA

Unit	Type
31 Escadrille	C–130H/H–30
32 Escadrille	C–130H/H–30
33 Escadrille	C–130H/H–30
35 Escadrille	C–130H/H–30

C-130H of the Algerian Air Force.

ARGENTINA

Unit	Type
1 Brigada Aerea	
1 Esquadron de Transport, BAM El Palomar, Buenos Aires	C-130B/E/H, KC-130H

AUSTRALIA

Unit	Type
No 86 Wing (Airlift Group)	
No 36 Squadron, Richmond, NSW	C-130H
No 37 Squadron, Richmond, NSW	C-130E

BAHRAIN

Unit	Type
Not known	C–130B

C-130H of the Argentine Air Force. PHOTO: PETER R. MARCH

BELGIUM

Unit	Type
Groupement de Transport/No 15 Wing	
20 Smaldeel, Brussels-Melsbroek	C-130H

BOLIVIA

Unit	Type
Transporte Aereo Boliviano	
Grupo Aereo de Transporte 71, BA General Walter Arze, La Paz	C-130A/B/H

BRAZIL

Unit	Type
1 Grupo de Transporte	
1 Esquadrao, Galeao Airport, Rio de Janeiro	C/KC-130H
2 Esquadrao, Galeao Airport, Rio de Janeiro	C/KC-130H
1 Grupo de Transporte de Tropas	
2 Esquadrao, BA dos Afonsos, Rio de Janeiro	C-130E

C-130H of 20 Smaldeel, Belgian Air Force wearing markings commemorating the unit's 20th anniversary. PHOTO: PETER R. MARCH

C-130H of the Brazilian Air Force.

CAMEROON

Not known	C-130H/H-30

CANADA

No 8 Wing	
No 424 Squadron, Trenton, Ontario	CC-130E/H
No 426 Squadron, Trenton, Ontario	CC-130E/H
No 429 Squadron, Trenton, Ontario	CC-130E/H
No 436 Squadron, Trenton, Ontario	CC-130E/H
No 14 Wing	
No 413 Squadron, Greenwood, Nova Scotia	CC-130E
No 18 Wing	
No 418 (Air Reserve) Squadron, Edmonton, Alberta	CC-130E/H
No 435 Squadron, Edmonton, Alberta	CC-130E/H/H(T)

CHAD

Not known	C-130A/H/H–30

CHILE

II Brigada/Ala 2	
Grupo de Aviacion 10, Santiago (Merino Benitez)	C-130B/H

COLOMBIA

Grupo de Transportes	
Escuadron de Transporte 711, Eldorado Airport, Bogota	C-130B/H

DENMARK

Eskadrille 721, Vaerlose	C-130H

C-130H (1001) of Colombian Air Force.

C-130H of Gabon Air Force based at Leon M'Ba Airport.

DUBAI/UAE
Transport Squadron, Mindhat — C-130H-30, L-100-30

ECUADOR
Ala de Transporte II, Mariscal Sucre AB, Quito — C-130B/H, L-100-30

EGYPT
Not known — C-130H/H–30

FRANCE
Escadre de Transport 61
Escadron de Transport 2/61, Orleans-Bricy — C-130H/H-30

GABON
Escadrille de Transport, Leon M'Ba Airport — C-130H, L-100-30

GREECE
112 Pterix
356 Mira, Elefsis — C-130B/H

HONDURAS
Escadrilla de Transporte, Tocontin Airport, Tegucigalpa — C-130A

INDONESIA
No 31 Squadron, Jakarta-Halim — C-130B/H
No 32 Squadron, Malang — C-130B/H/H-30/L–100–30

IRAN
Not known — C-130E/H

C-130H 5-149 of the (then) Imperial Iranian Air Force visiting Muscat in November 1975.

ISRAEL
No 131 Squadron, Lod Airport, Tel Aviv — C-130E/H, KC-130H

Italian AF C-130Hs are operated from Pisa by 50 Gruppo of 46 Aerobrigata PHOTO: PETER R. MARCH

ITALY
46 Aerobrigata
50 Gruppo, Pisa-San Giusto C-130H

JAPAN
1st Tactical Airlift Group
401 Squadron, Komaki AB C-130H

Japanese Air Force/Defence Force C-130H (85-1079) taking part in exercises at Pope AFB, North Carolina. PHOTO: LINDSAY PEACOCK

The Royal Netherlands Air Force is the latest operator of the C-130H.

JORDAN
No 3 Squadron, Amman-King Abdullah C-130B/H

KUWAIT
No 41 Squadron, Kuwait International Airport L-100-30

LIBYA
Not known C-130H, L-100-20/30

MALAYSIA
No 4 Squadron, Kuala Lumpur (Subang) C-130H-MP
No 14 Squadron, Kuala Lumpur (Subang) C-130H/H–30

MEXICO
6 Gruppo Aereo
Escuadron Aereo Transporte Pesado 302, Santa Lucia C-130A

MOROCCO
Unit not known, Kenitra C-130H, KC-130H

NETHERLANDS
No 334 Squadron, Eindhoven C-130H-30

NEW ZEALAND
Operations Wing
No 40 Squadron, Whenuapai C-130H

NIGER
Not known C-130H

NIGERIA
Unit not known, Lagos Airport C-130H/H–30

NORWAY
335 Skvadron, Gardermoen C-130H

OMAN
No 4 Squadron, Muscat-Seeb Airport C-130B/H

PAKISTAN
No 35 (Composite) Air Transport Wing
No 6 Squadron, Chaklala AB C-130B/E, L-100
Transport Conversion School, Chaklala AB (loaned from above)

PERU
Grupe Aereo de Transporte 8
Escuadron 841, Jorge Chavez Airport, Lima C-130A/B, L-100-20

PHILIPPINES
220 Heavy Airlift Wing
222 Heavy Airlift Squadron, Mactan C-130B/H/L–100–20

PORTUGAL
Esquadra de Transporte 501, Montijo C-130H/H-30

SAUDI ARABIA
No 1 Squadron, Riyadh VC-130H
No 4 Squadron, Jeddah C-130E/H/H-30, KC-130H
No 16 Squadron, Jeddah C-130E/H/H-30, KC-130H

SINGAPORE
No 122 Squadron, Paya Lebar C-130H, KC-130B/H

SOUTH AFRICA
No 28 Squadron, Waterkloof C-130B

SOUTH KOREA
Air Transport Wing, Pusan C-130H/H-30

SPAIN
Ala de Transporte 31
Escuadron 311, Zaragoza C-130H/H-30, KC-130H
Escuadron 312, Zaragoza C-130H/H-30, KC-130H

SUDAN
Not known C-130H

SWEDEN
Flygflottilj 7
Transportflygdivisionen, Satenas — C-130H

TAIWAN
No 6 Troop Carrier and Anti-Submarine Combined Wing
No 101 Squadron, Pingtung — C-130H

THAILAND
No 6 Wing
No 601 Squadron, Bangkok-Don Muang — C-130H/H-30

TUNISIA
Escadrille de Transport et Communication, Bizerta — C-130H

TURKEY
222 Filo, Erkilet/Kayseri — C-130B/E

UGANDA
Not known — L–100–20

UNITED KINGDOM

No 24 Squadron, RAF Lyneham	Hercules C1P/C3P
No 30 Squadron, RAF Lyneham	Hercules C1P/C3P
No 47 Squadron, RAF Lyneham	Hercules C1P/C3P
No 57 (Reserve) Squadron, RAF Lyneham	Hercules C1P/C3P
No 70 Squadron, RAF Lyneham	Hercules C1P/C3P
No 1312 Flight, Mount Pleasant	Hercules C1K
Meteorological Research Flight, Farnborough	Hercules W2

C-130H (Z-21012/TS-MTB) of the Tunisian Air Force.

All of the Lyneham based Hercules variants in formation: C1P at the front and rear; C3Ps on each wing and a C1K in the centre.
PHOTO: PETER R. MARCH

UNITED STATES AIR FORCE

Wing/Group	*Base*	*Squadron(s)*	*Variant(s)*
Air Combat Command			
1 FW/Wg	Langley, VA (at Patrick, FL)	71 RQS	HC-130P
7 Wg	Dyess, TX	39/40 ALS	C-130H
23 Wg	Pope, NC	2/41 ALS	C-130E
24 Wg	Howard, Canal Zone	310 ALS	C-130H
314 AW	Little Rock, AR	50/53/61/62 ALS	C- 130E/H
355 Wg	Davis-Monthan, AZ	41/43 ECS	EC-130H
552 ACW	Tinker, OK (at Keesler, MS)	7 ACCS	EC-130E, C-130H
Pacific Air Forces			
3 Wg	Elmendorf, AK	517 ALS	C-130H
374 AW	Yokota, Japan	36 ALS	C-130E/H
United States Air Forces in Europe			
435 AW	Rhein-Main, Germany	37 ALS	C-130E
Air Force Special Operations Command			
16 SOW	Hurlburt Field, FL	8 SOS	MC-130E, C-130E
	Eglin, FL	9 SOS	HC-130N/P
	Hurlburt Field, FL	15 SOS	MC-130H
	Hurlburt Field, FL	16 SOS	AC-130H
352 SOG	Alconbury, England	7 SOS	MC-130H
		67 SOS	HC-130N/P, C-130E
353 SOG	Kadena, Okinawa	1 SOS	MC-130E
		17 SOS	HC-130N/P
Air Education and Training Command			
542 CTW	Kirtland, NM	550 ATS	HC-130N/P, MC-130H
Air Force Materiel Command			
412 TW	Edwards, CA	418 TS	AC-130U, MC-130H
545 TG	Hill, UT	514 TS	DC-130A, C-130B, HC/NC-130H

US AIR FORCE RESERVE

Wing/Group	Base	Squadron(s)	Variant(s)
94 AW/94 OG	Dobbins, GA	700 ALS	C-130H
94 AW/911 AG	Grtr Pittsburgh, PA	758 ALS	C-130H
94 AW/914 AG	Niagara Falls, NY	328 ALS	C-130H
302 AW/302 OG	Peterson, CO	731 ALS	C-130H
302 AW/934 AG	Minn-St Paul, MN	96 ALS	C-130E
403 AW/403 OG	Keesler, MS	815 ALS	C-130E/H, WC-130E/H
403 AW/908 AG	Maxwell, AL	357 ALS	C-130H
403 AW/913 AG	Willow Grove, PA	327 ALS	C-130E
440 AW/440 OG	Gen Mitchell Fd, WI	95 ALS	C-130H
440 AW/910 AG	Youngstown, OH	757 ALS	C-130H

C-130E (68-10935) of the 37 ALS/435 AW. PHOTO: SUE J. BUSHELL

North Carolina Air Guard C-130H from 145 AG/156 ALS based at Douglas International Airport, demonstrating the Modular Airborne Fire Fighting System (MAFFS). PHOTO: JOHN DUNNELL

440 AW/928 AG	Chicago/O'Hare, IL	64 ALS	C-130H
445 AW/943 AG	March, CA	303 ALS	C-130B/E
919 SOW/919 OG	Duke Field, FL	711 SOS	AC-130A
939 RQW/939 OG	Portland, OR	304 RQS	HC-130P
939 RQW/RQG	Patrick, FL	301 RQS	HC-130N

AIR NATIONAL GUARD

102 RQS	Suffolk County, NY	106 RQG	HC-130P
105 ALS	Nashville, TN	118 AW	C-130H
109 ALS	Minn-St Paul, MN	133 AW	C-130E
115 ALS	Point Mugu, CA	146 AW	C-130E
129 RQS	Moffett Field, CA	129 RQG	HC-130P
130 ALS	Charleston, WV	130 AG	C-130H
135 ALS	Baltimore, MD	135 AG	C-130E
139 ALS	Stratton ANGB, NY	109 AG	C/LC-130H
142 ALS	Wilmington, DE	166 AG	C-130H
143 ALS	Quonset Pt, RI	143 AG	C-130E
144 ALS	Kulis ANGB, AK	176 CG	C-130H
154 TS	Little Rock, AR	189 AG	C-130E
156 ALS	Douglas IAP, NC	145 AG	C-130H
158 ALS	Savannah, GA	165 AG	C-130H
164 ALS	Mansfield, OH	179 AG	C-130H
165 ALS	Louisville, KY	123 AW	C-130H
167 ALS	Martinsburg, WV	167 AG	C-130E
171 ALS	Selfridge ANGB, MI	191 AG	C-130E
180 ALS	St Joseph, MO	139 AG	C-130H
181 ALS	Dallas, TX	136 AW	C-130H
185 ALS	Oklahoma City, OK	137 AW	C-130H
187 ALS	Cheyenne, WY	153 AG	C-130H
193 SOS	Harrisburg, PA	193 SOG	EC-130E
210 RQS	Kulis ANGB, AK	176 CG	HC-130H(N)

Operational Support Aircraft

122 FS	New Orleans, LA	159 FG	C-130H
157 FS	McEntire ANGB, SC	169 FG	C-130H
160 FS	Montgomery, AL	187 FG	C-130H

Notes: The 171 ALS/191 AG is due to transition from the F-16A/B to the C-130E in mid-1994. Those units that utilise the C-130H as an Operational Support Aircraft (OSA) possess only one example. It is likely that the few OSA aircraft that remain will soon be replaced by C-26Bs and re-assigned.

UNITED STATES NAVY

Unit	*Base*	*Variant*
VRC-50	Agana NAS, Guam	C-130F
VR-53	Washington NAF, MD	C-130T
VR-54	New Orleans NAS, LA	C-130T
VXE-6	Point Mugu NAS, CA	LC-130F/R
Blue Angels	Pensacola NAS, FL	TC-130G
Adak	Adak NAS, AK	KC-130F

UNITED STATES MARINE CORPS

Unit	*Base*	*Variant*
VMGR-152	Futenma MCAS, Okinawa	KC-130F
VMGR-234	Glenview NAS, IL	KC-130T/T-30
VMGR-252	Cherry Point MCAS, NC	KC-130F/R
VMGRT-253	Cherry Point MCAS, NC	KC-130F
VMGR-352	El Toro MCAS, CA	KC-130F/R
VMGR-452	Stewart Field, NY	KC-130T/T-30

UNITED STATES COAST GUARD

Coast Guard Air Station	*Variant*
Barber's Point, HI	HC-130H
Borinquen, Puerto Rico	HC-130H
Clearwater, FL	HC-130H, EC-130V
Elizabeth City, NC	HC-130H
Kodiak, AK	HC-130H
Sacramento, CA	HC-130H

URUGUAY
Brigada Aerea I
Regimento Tactico 1, Montevideo-Carrasco — C-130B

VENEZUELA
Grupo Aereo de Transporte 6
Escuadron T1, El Libertador, Palo Negro, Maracay — C-130H

YEMEN
Not known — C-130H

ZAIRE
19 Wing d'Appui Logistique
191 Escadrille, N'Djili Airport, Kinshasa — C-130H

C-130H of the Venezuelan Air Force. PHOTO: R. R. LEADER

NON–US MILITARY OPERATORS BY COUNTRY AND VARIANT

	C-130A	*C-130B*	*C-130E*	*C-130H*	*C-130H-MP*	*C-130H-30*	*KC-130H*	*C-130K*	*L-100*
Abu Dhabi				★					
Algeria				★		★			
Argentina		☆	★	★			★		
Australia	★		★	★					
Bahrain		☆							
Belgium				★					
Bolivia	☆	☆		★					
Brazil			★	★			★		
Cameroon				★		★			
Canada		★	★	★					
Chad	☆			★		★			
Chile		☆		★					
Colombia		☆		★					
Denmark				★					
Dubai				★					★
Ecuador		☆		★					★
Egypt				★		★			
France				★		★			
Gabon				★					★
Greece		☆		★					
Honduras	☆								
Indonesia		★		★	★	★			★
Iran		★	★	★					
Israel		☆		★			★		
Italy				★					
Japan				★					
Jordan		☆		★					
Kuwait									★
Libya				★					☆
Malaysia				★	★	★			
Mexico	☆								
Morocco				★			★		
Netherlands				★					
New Zealand				★					
Niger				★					
Nigeria				★		★			
Norway				★					
Oman		☆		★					
Pakistan		★	☆						☆
Peru	☆	☆							★
Philippines		☆		★					☆
Portugal				★		★			
Saudi Arabia			★	★		★	★		★
Singapore		☆		★			★		
South Africa		★							
South Korea				★		★			
South Vietnam	☆								
Spain				★		★	★		
Sudan				★					
Sweden			★	★					
Taiwan				★					
Thailand				★		★			
Tunisia				★					
Turkey		☆	★						
Uganda									☆
United Kingdom								★	
Uruguay		☆							
Venezuela				★					
Yemen				★					
Zaire				★					

Key ★=Delivered new to customer ☆=Acquired second-hand
Note: This table details past and present users and lists information on all variants used by the countries detailed. Some of the models are no longer in service.

APPENDIX G
CIVIL OPERATORS OF THE C-130/L-100 HERCULES

Algeria	
Air Algerie, Algiers	L-100-30
Angola	
Angola Air Charter, Luanda	L-100-30
TAAG Angolan Airlines, Luanda	L-100-30
Argentina	
Lineas Aereas de Estado (LADE), Buenos Aires	L-100-30
Canada	
Canadian Airlines International, Vancouver	L-100-30
Northwest Territorial Airways, Yellowknife	L-100-30 (leased)
China	
China Air Cargo, Shanxi	L-100-30
Ethiopia	
Ethiopian Airlines, Addis Ababa	L-100-30
France	
EAS Air Cargo, Perpignan	L-100-30
Gabon	
Air Gabon, Libreville	L-100-30
Indonesia	
Merpati Nusantara Airlines, Jakarta	L-100-30
Pelita Air Service, Jakarta	L-100-30
Libya	
Jamahiriya Air Transport, Tripoli	L-100-20/30
Mexico	
Aeropostal, Mexico City	C-130A
Petroleos Mexicanos (Pemex), Mexico City	L-100-30
Netherlands	
Schreiner Airways, Leiden	L-100-30 (leased)
Netherlands Antilles	
Frameair	L-100-30
Philippines	
Aboitiz Air Transport	C-130A
Sao Tome	
Transafrik, Sao Tome	L-100-20/30
Saudi Arabia	
Saudia, Jeddah	L-100-30
South Africa	
Safair Freighter (Pty) Ltd, Johannesburg	L-100-30
Uganda	
Uganda Air Cargo, Kampala	L-100-30
United States of America	
Advanced Leasing Corp	L-100-30
Aero Firefighting Services, Anaheim, CA	C-130A
African Cargo Inc., Miami, FL	C-130A
Butler Aircraft Co., Redmond OR	C-130A
Flight Cargo Leasing Inc., Dover, NY	L-100-30
Hemet Valley Flying Service Inc., Hemet, CA	C-130A
IEP IEPO, Chatsworth, CA	C-130A
Military Aircraft Restoration Corp, Anaheim, CA	C-130A
National Aeronautics and Space Administration,	
Moffett Field, CA	NC-130B
Wallops Island, VA	EC-130Q
National Oceanic & Atmospheric Administration,	
Miami, FL	L-100-30, EC-130Q
National Science Foundation	EC-130Q
Pacific Gateway Investments, Orange, CA	C-130A
Pacific Harbor Capital Inc., Portland, OR	C-130A
Pegasus Aviation Co	L-100-30
Rapid Air Trans, Washington, DC	L-100-30
Snow Aviation International Inc., Columbus, OH	C-130A
Southern Air Transport, Miami, FL	L-100-20/30
T&G Aviation, Chandler, AZ	C-130A
TBM Inc., Redmond, OR	C-130A
World Wide Trading Inc., Delray Beach, FL	L-100-30
Yemen	
Yemenia, Sanaa	C-130H
GOVERNMENT AND AIR FORCE OPERATED L–100s	
Government of Dubai	L-100-30
Government of Ecuador	L-100-30
Republic of Gabon	L-100-30
Indonesian Air Force	L-100-30
Republic of Indonesia	L-100-30
Pakistan Air Force	L–100
Kuwait Air Force	L-100-30
Peruvian Air Force	L-100-20
Philippine Air Force	L-100-20
Republic of Uganda	L-100-30

Not surprisingly, Southern Air Transport has a large fleet of L-100-30s. PHOTO: ANDREW MARCH

Titles available in this series:–

01 INTERNATIONAL AIR TATTOO 93 –
The world's largest military air show
Published October 1993
ISBN 0-9516581-4-X
Price £10.95

02 MIGHTY HERCULES –
The first four decades
Published July 1994
ISBN 0-9516581-6-6
Price £14.95

03 INTERNATIONAL AIR TATTOO 94
Published October 1994
ISBN 0-9516581-7-4
Price £10.95

04 ROYAL AIR FORCE ALMANAC
Published October 1994
ISBN 0-9516581-8-2
Price £14.95

These books are available from RAF Benevolent Fund Enterprises Publishing, Building 15, RAF Fairford, Glos GL7 4DL, England. For postage add for each publication £1.50 UK; £2.50 Europe; £3 Outside Europe by Surface Mail. Send IMO or Sterling cheque drawn on UK Bank payable to RAFBF Enterprises or charge made against Visa or Mastercard – please quote Card No, name of bearer and expiry date.